JOSH　独一无二

JOSH DUYIWUER

TERRY WALTZ

SQUID FOR BRAINS
ALBANY, NY

Josh Duyiwuer
Terry Waltz
Published by Squid For Brains
Albany, NY
Copyright ©2014 by Terry T. Waltz

ISBN-10: 0615972519

ISBN-13: 978-0615972510

Chapter One

砰砰砰!

我用手打了 储物柜。我用力打了几次，但是都没办法。

砰砰砰!

我再打了几次。我的手痛了。我的腿也痛了。为什麽没有人听到?

我什麽都看不见。不要哭! 他们要我哭。但是为什麽他们要这个样子?

砰砰砰!

我开始用脚踢了。我小的时候，我踢橄榄球踢得很多，所以我很会踢。我用力踢了三四次，然後再用手打。我要打几次，才会有人听到呢?

我开始累了。我再打三次，砰砰砰，然後我就不打了。我太累了。就是太累了! 虽然我打了很多次，但是都没有办法。没有人听到。我要等。我要等到人走到我这儿。没办法。

我看了前面。黑、黑、再黑。比晚上十二点钟还要黑。我什麽都看不见。

dìyīzhāng

pēngpēngpēng!

wǒ yòngshǒu dǎle chǔwùguì. wǒ yònglì dǎle jǐcì, dànshì dōu méibànfǎ.

pēngpēngpēng!

wǒ zài dǎle jǐcì. wǒde shǒu tòngle. wǒde tuǐ yě tòngle. wèishénme méiyǒu rén tīngdào?

wǒ shénme dōu kànbújiàn. búyào kū! tāmen yào wǒ kū. dànshì wèishénme tāmen yào zhège yàngzi?

pēngpēngpēng!

wǒ kāishǐ yòng jiǎo tīle. wǒ xiǎo deshíhòu, wǒ tī gǎnlǎnqiú tīde hěnduō, suǒyǐ wǒ hěnhuì tī. wǒ yònglì tīle sānsìcì, ránhòu zài yòngshǒu dǎ. wǒ yào dǎ jǐcì, cái huì yǒu rén tīngdào ne?

wǒ kāishǐ lèile. wǒ zài dǎ sāncì, pēngpēngpēng, ránhòu wǒ jiù bùdǎle. wǒ tàilèile. jiùshì tàilèile! suīrán wǒ dǎle hěnduō cì, dànshì dōu méiyǒubànfǎ. méiyǒu rén tīngdào. wǒ yào děng. wǒ yào děngdào rén zǒu dào wǒ zhèr. méibànfǎ.

wǒ kànle qiánmiàn. hēi, hēi, zài hēi. bǐ wǎnshàng shíèrdiǎnzhōng háiyào hēi. wǒ shénme dōu kànbújiàn. wǒ hěn xiǎng kàndào

6

我很想看到东西，但是这里太黑了。想吧！有什麼东西可以用？在这儿都有什麼？

但是虽然东西很多（有我的背包、很多课本、笔、钱包等）但是我都看不见。我的手也很通。我要拿东西打储物柜，但是我拿不到。

怎麼没有人来？几点钟了？六点了吗？七点了吗？晚上有人来学校学法语、画画。他们到的时候，他们会听到。但是我要等多久？我的腿很痛！

我很烦恼。我烦恼得快要哭了。我很想吃饭。我很想在家做功课。虽然我不喜欢做功课，但是在家做功课比在这儿等好多了。在这儿等比化学课还要无聊。都是看不见，拿不到东西，头痛手痛腿痛的麻烦！

砰砰砰！

我等了三四十分钟以後，才听到了两个人来。一个男人、一个女人。我听他们来，但是我听不懂他们在说什麼。

我虽然累了，但是我很想回家。

砰砰砰！

dōngxī. dànshì zhèlǐ tàihēile. xiǎng ba! yǒu
shénme dōngxī kěyǐ yòng? zài zhèr dōu yǒu
shénme?

dànshì suīrán dōngxī hěnduō (yǒu wǒde
bēibāo, hěnduō kèběn, bǐ, qiánbāoděng) dànshì
wǒ dōu kànbújiàn. wǒde shǒu yě hěn tòng. wǒ
yào ná dōngxī dǎ chǔwùguì, dànshì wǒ nábúdào.

zěnme méiyǒurén lái? jǐdiǎnzhōng le? liùdiǎn
le ma? qīdiǎn le ma? wǎnshàng yǒurén lái
xuéxiào xué fǎyǔ, huàhuà. tāmen dào deshíhòu,
tāmen huì tīngdào. dànshì wǒ yào děng duōjiǔ?
wǒde tuǐ hěn tòng!

wǒ hěn fánnǎo. wǒ fánnǎo de kuàiyào kūle.
wǒ hěn xiǎng chīfàn. wǒ hěn xiǎng zàijiā zuò
gōngkè. suīrán wǒ bù xǐhuān zuò gōngkè,
dànshì zàijiā zuò gōngkè bǐ zàizhèr děng hǎoduō
le. zài zhèr děng bǐ huàxuékè háiyào wúliáo.
dōushì kànbújiàn, nábúdào dōngxī, tóutòng
shǒutòng tuǐtòng de máfán!

pēngpēngpēng!

wǒ děngle sānsìshífēnzhōng yǐhòu, cái
tīngdàole liǎngge rén lái. yīge nánrén, yīge
nǔrén. wǒ tīng tāmen lái, dànshì wǒ tīngbùdǒng
tāmen shuō shénme.

wō suīrán lèile, dànshì wǒ hěnxiǎng huíjiā.

pēngpēngpēng!

「什麼？你听到了吗？」

砰砰砰！砰砰砰！「我在这儿！」

「是那个储物柜吧！」

「是的！我在这儿！」他们听到了！

「储物柜在说话吗？」

我很烦恼。我等了这麼久。那两个人怎麼那麼笨？

还好女人没有那个男人笨。「不是！里面有人吧。」她的英文有一点特别。

「有人吗？你在哪儿？」

「六三五号！快打开吧！」砰砰砰！我再打了几次。

男人说：「我要用什麼号码打开？」

「二十八、四、三十二。」

「二十八、四…多少？」

「三十二！三十二！」那个男人有多笨呢？

「好了，好了，不要烦恼，我在打开！」

我听了一个「砰」，然後门就开了。外面不黑。我的眼睛痛了。我很高兴，

"shénme? nǐ tīngdàole ma?"

pēngpēngpēng! pēngpēngpēng! "wǒ zài zhèr!"

"shì nàge chǔwùguì ba!"

"shìde! wǒ zài zhèr!" tāmen tīngdàole!

"chǔwùguì zài shuōhuà ma?"

wǒ hěn fánnǎo. wǒ děngle zhème jiǔ. nà liǎngge rén zěnme nàme bèn?

háihǎo nǚrén méiyǒu nàge nánrén bèn. "búshì! lǐmiàn yǒu rén ba." tāde yīngwén yǒu yīdiǎn tèbié.

"yǒu rén ma? nǐ zài nǎěr?"

"liùsānwǔ hào! kuài dǎkāi ba!" pēngpēngpēng! wǒ zài dǎle jǐcì.

nánrén shuō: "wǒ yào yòng shénme hàomǎ dǎkāi?"

"èrshíbā, sì, sānshíèr."

"èrshíbā, sì ... duōshǎo?"

"sānshíèr! sānshíèr!" nàge nánrén yǒu duō bèn ne?

"hǎole, hǎole, búyào fánnǎo, wǒ zài dǎkāi!"

wǒ tīngle yīge "pēng", ránhòu mén jiù kāile.

wàimiàn bù hēi. wǒde yǎnjīng tòngle. wǒ

因为我在储物柜外了。我们学校的储物柜不大。

我看了看两个人。那个男人是英文老师。但是还有一个女孩子。一个很好看的女孩子。我的脸红了。好看的女孩子看了我在储物柜里面。不好意思！

老师跟我说：「Josh，你为什麼在储物柜里面呢？」

我很烦恼。我不想跟他说我为什麼在储物柜里面。太不好意思了！他如果不懂，我就不想跟他说。特别是，因为「她」在！

那个男人说：「没有关係。快五点了！」女孩子再看了我一眼就跟他走了。

我的腿还很痛。我在储物柜很久。但是我都不在想我的腿了。那天，我都在想那个女孩子。她是谁？

hěn gāoxìng, yīnwèi wǒ zài chǔwùguì wài le.
wǒmen xuéxiào de chǔwùguì búdà.

wǒ kànlekàn liǎngge rén. nàge nánrén shì
yīngwén lǎoshī. dànshì háiyǒu yīge nǚháizǐ.
yīge hěnhǎokàn de nǚháizǐ. wǒde liǎn hóngle.
hǎokànde nǚháizǐ kànle wǒ zài chǔwùguì
lǐmiàn. bùhǎoyìsi!

lǎoshī gēnwǒ shuō: "Josh, nǐ wéishénme zài
chǔwùguì lǐmiàn ne?"

wǒ hěn fánnǎo. wǒ bùxiǎng gēn tā shuō wǒ
wèishénme zài chǔwùguì lǐmiàn. tài bùhǎoyìsi
le! tā rúguǒ bùdǒng, wǒ jiù bùxiǎng gēn tā shuō.
tèbié shì, yīnwèi "tā" zài!

nàge nánrén shuō: "méiyǒu guānxi. kuài
wǔdiǎn le!" nǚháizǐ zài kànle wǒ yīyǎn jiù gēntā
zǒu le.

wǒde tuǐ hái hěn tòng. wǒ zài chǔwùguì
hěnjiǔ. dànshì wǒ dōu búzài xiǎng wǒde tuǐ le.
nàtiān, wǒ dōu zàixiǎng nàge nǚháizǐ. tā shì
shéi?

Chapter Two

不好意思，我都没有自我介绍！

我的名字叫 Josh。以前，我都很高兴。但是今年就不一样了。

我的家在 New York。你在想 New York City，对不对？但是我们的家在 Schoharie。Schoharie 地方大，但是人少。是很无聊的地方。

虽然地方小，但是我的家还不错。我们的家是农场。我爸爸养牛，所以我们都养牛。养牛的工作很多。我去学校以前，都要去给牛挤奶。还好我们不用手挤奶。爸爸买了很好的挤奶机。虽然挤奶机很好用，但是我们还要小心。有的时候牛还会踢人。

我不是很喜欢牛。爸爸也养猪、三四十只鸡、还有狗和猫。爸爸很喜欢牛，因为他们不说话。爸爸说，牛跟人不一样，因为人都说话说得太多了。

今年我是九年级的学生。中文要说「高一」，因为美国的九年级就是中国的

dìèrzhāng

bùhǎoyìsi! wǒ dōu méiyǒu zìwǒjièshào!

wǒde míngzǐ jiào Josh. yǐqián, wǒ dōu hěn gāoxìng. dànshì jīnnián jiù bù yíyàng le.

wǒde jiā zài New York. nǐ zàixiǎng New York City, duìbúduì? dànshì wǒmen de jiā zài Schoharie. Schoharie dìfāng dà, dànshì rén shǎo. shì hěn wúliáo de dìfāng.

suīrán dìfāng xiǎo, dànshì wǒde jiā hái búcuò. wǒmen de jiā shì nóngchǎng. wǒ bàba yǎngniú, suǒyǐ wǒmen dōu yǎngniú. yǎngniú de gōngzuò hěnduō. wǒ qù xuéxiào yǐqián, dōu yào qù gěiniú jǐnǎi. háihǎo wǒmen bú yòng shǒu jǐnǎi. bàba mǎile hěnhǎo de jǐnǎijī. suīrán jǐnǎijī hěn hǎoyòng, dànshì wǒmen háiyào xiǎoxīn. yǒude shíhòu niú háihuì tīrén.

wǒ búshì hěn xǐhuān niú. bàba yě yǎng zhū, sānsìshí zhī jī, háiyǒu gǒu hé māo. bàba hěn xǐhuān niú, yīnwèi tāmen bù shuōhuà. bàba shuō, niú gēn rén bù yíyàng, yīnwèi rén dōu shuōhuà shuōde tàiduōle.

jīnnián wǒ shì jiǔniánjí de xuéshēng. zhongwén yào shuō "gāoyī", yīnwèi měiguó de jiǔniánjí jiùshì zhōngguó de gāoyī. dànshì wǒ

高一。 但是 我 在 美国, 所以 我 说「九年级」。 (老师 在 看 吗? 哈哈!)

我们 的 高中 不错。 老师们 也 不错。 很多 老师 都 是 我 爸爸 妈妈 的 好 朋友。 很多 Schoharie 的 人 都 是 我 父母 的 朋友, 因为 Schoharie 地方 不大。 Schoharie 的 人 不多, 所以 他们 都 是 朋友。

我 有 一个 不错 的 妈妈。 她 做 的 饭 都 很 好吃。 她 都 在家。 有 一天 我 跟 她 说, 「还好 你 不用 工作, 不是 很 好 吗?」 她 很 生 我 的 气。 她 说, 如果 我 不想 农场 的 工作 很多, 她 还有 工作 要 我 做。 以後 我 都 没有 跟 她 说「不 工作」了!

我 的 爸爸 也 不错。 他 都 在 农场 工作。 农场 的 工作 很多, 所以 我 跟 我 哥哥 也 要 跟 爸爸 妈妈 在 农场 工作。 虽然 牛 很 麻烦, 但是 我 喜欢 我们 的 农场。

我 的 哥哥 也 不错。 他 叫 Jared。 今年 他 是 十二年级 的 学生。 (我 错 了! 他 是「高四」学生 了。) Jared 说, 高四 的 功课 那麽 多, 他 是「搞死」的 学生。 Jared 不 喜欢 功课。

他 很 喜欢 在 农场 工作。 但是 虽然 他 不 喜欢, 他 功课 都 做得 很 好。 如果 我 是 高

zài měiguó, suǒyǐ wǒ shuō"jiǔniánjí". (lǎoshī zài kàn ma? hāhā!)

wǒmen de gāozhōng búcuò. lǎoshīmen yě búcuò. hěnduō láoshī dōu shì wǒ bàba māma de hǎo péngyǒu. hěnduō Schoharie de rén dōu shì wǒ fùmǔ de péngyǒu, yīnwèi Schoharie dìfāng búdà. Schoharie de rén bù duō, suǒyǐ tāmen dōu shì péngyǒu.

wǒ yǒu yīge búcuò de māma. tā zuòdefàn dōu hěn hǎochī. tā dōu zài jiā. yǒu yītiān wǒ gēntāshuō, "háihǎo nǐ búyòng gōngzuò, búshì hěn hǎoma?" tā hěn shēng wǒde qì. tā shuō, rúguǒ wǒ bù xiǎng nóngchǎng de gōngzuò hěnduō, tā háiyǒu gōngzuò yào wǒ zuò. yǐhòu wǒ dōu méiyǒu gēn tā shuō "bù gōngzuò" le!

wǒde bàba yě búcuò. tā dōu zài nóngchǎng gōngzuò. nóngchǎng de gōngzuò hěnduō. suǒyǐ wǒ gēn wǒ gēge yě yào gēn bàba māma zài nóngchǎng gōngzuò. suīrán niú hěn máfán, dànshì wǒ xǐhuān wǒmen de nóngchǎng.

wǒde gēge yě búcuò. tā jiào Jared. jīnnián tā shì shíèrniánjí de xuéshēng. (wǒ cuòle! tā shì "gāosì" xuéshēng le.) Jared shuō, gāosì de gōngkè nàme duō, tā shì "gǎosǐ" de xuéshēng. Jared bù xǐhuān gōngkè.

tā hěn xǐhuān nóngchǎng gōngzuò. dànshì suīrán tā bù xǐhuān, tā gōngkè dōu zuòde

四 的 学生，我 都 不会 做 功课 了。高四 的 时候，有 什麽 用？

Jared 什么 都 做得 很好。他 在 学校 打 篮球。他 也 踢 橄榄球。他 橄榄球、篮球 都 很好。他的 朋友 也 很多。在 学校，人人 都 喜欢 他。他的 朋友 不是 打 篮球 就是 踢 橄榄球。

我 哥哥 也 有 女朋友。他的 女朋友 叫 Lauren。Lauren 很 好看。她 很 高。她 在 学校 打 篮球。大家 都 说，Jared 跟 Lauren 很 好看。

你 在 想，我 为什麽 不 高兴 吗？我的 家人 很好，农场 不错，有 什麽 不好 呢？没错，很多 人 都 会 这麽 想。但是 我 有 一个 很大 的 问题。

我 太矮 了。

好了，现在 你 知道，我 为什麽 在 储物柜 里面。是 因为 我的 同学。我的 很高的 同学。

以前 都 没有 问题。我 小 的 时候，高不高 都 没有 关系。我的 爸爸 很高。我 哥哥 长高 了。妈妈 说，我 也 会 长得 很高。我 七年级 的 时候，我的 朋友 都 开始 长高。

hěnhǎo. rúguǒ wǒ shì gāosì de xuéshēng, wǒ dōu búhuì zuò gōngkè le. gāosì deshíhòu, yǒu shénme yòng?

Jared shénme dōu zuòde hěnhǎo. tā zài xuéxiào dǎ lánqiú. tā yě tī gǎnlǎnqiú. tā gǎnlǎnqiú, lánqiú dōu hěnhǎo. tāde péngyǒu yě hěnduō. zài xuéxiào, rénrén dōu xǐhuān tā. tāde péngyǒu búshì dǎ lánqiú jiùshì tī gǎnlǎnqiú.

wǒ gēge yě yǒu nǚpéngyǒu. tāde nǚpéngyǒu jiào Lauren. Lauren hěn hǎokàn. tā hěn gāo. tā zài xuéxiào dǎ lánqiú. dàjiā dōu shuō, Jared gēn Lauren hěn hǎokàn.

nǐ zàixiǎng, wǒ wèishénme bù gāoxìng ma? wǒde jiārén hěnhǎo, nóngchǎng búcuò, yǒu shénme bùhǎo ne? méicuò, hěnduō rén dōu huì zhème xiǎng. dànshì wǒ yǒu yīge hěndà de wèntí.

wǒ tàiǎile.

hǎole, xiànzài nǐ zhīdào, wǒ wéishénme zài chǔwùguì lǐmiàn. shì yīnwèi wǒde tóngxué. wǒde hěngāode tóngxué.

yǐqián dōu méiyǒu wèntí. wǒ xiǎo deshíhòu, gāobùgāo dōu méiyǒu guānxi. wǒde bàba hěngāo. wǒ gege zhǎnggāo le. māma shuō, wǒ yě huì zhǎngde hěngāo. wǒ qīniánjí deshíhòu, wǒde péngyǒu dōu kāishǐ zhǎnggāo. tāmen

他们一个月比一个月高。但是我都没有高了。我哥哥是橄榄球大明星。但是我呢？

八年级，同学都比我高。他们不喜欢我了。我不知道为什麼。他们以前也都矮。他们怎麼不懂，高矮没有关係？但是他们不懂。八年级，没有同学喜欢我了。

九年级的第一天，我就在储物柜里面。两个人开了储物柜以後，我就去看教练。我跟他说：「我很想踢橄榄球。我哥哥踢得很好。我也要学。」

教练看了看我。「你是…?」

「我是 Jared 的弟弟。」

他再看了我一眼。「Jared 的弟弟？你怎麼那麼…」

我们的学校很小。要踢橄榄球的人不多。教练怎麼说我不行？

「不好意思」他跟我说。「你就是太矮了。你哥哥踢得很好…但是…」他很不高兴地跟我说：「不好意思。你不行。」

那就是九年级的第一天。那个时候，我想不踢橄榄球是很大的问题。但是我

yīgeyuè bǐ yīgeyuè gāo. dànshì wǒ dōu méiyǒu gāole. wǒ gège shì gǎnlǎnqiú dà míngxīng. dànshì wǒ ne?

bāniánjí, tóngxué dōu bǐ wǒ gāo. tāmen bù xǐhuān wǒ le. wǒ bù zhīdào wèishénme. tāmen yǐqián yě dōu ǎi. tāmen zěnme bùdǒng. gāoǎi méiyǒu guānxi? dànshì tāmen bùdǒng. bāniánjí, méiyǒu tóngxué xǐhuān wǒ le.

jiǔniánjí de dìyītiān, wǒ jiù zài chǔwùguì lǐmiàn. liǎngge rén kāile chǔwùguì yǐhòu, wǒ jiù qù kàn jiàoliàn. wǒ gēn tā shuō: "wǒ hěnxiǎng tī gǎnlǎnqiú. wǒ gège tīde hěnhǎo. wǒ yě yào xué.

jiàoliàn kànlekàn wǒ. "nǐ shì...?"

"wǒ shì Jared de dìdi."

tā zài kànle wǒ yīyǎn. "Jared de dìdi? nǐ zěnme nàme..."

wǒmen de xuéxiào hěnxiǎo. yào tīgǎnlǎnqiú de rén bùduō. jiàoliàn zěnme shuō wǒ bùxíng?

"bùhǎoyìsi" tā gēn wǒ shuō. "nǐ jiùshì tàiǎile. nǐ gège tīde hěnhǎo...dànshì..." tā hěn bùgāoxìngde gēnwǒshuō: "bùhǎoyìsi... nǐ bùxíng."

nà jiùshì jiǔniánjí de dìyītiān. nàge shíhòu, wǒ xiǎng bùtīgǎnlǎnqiú shì hěndà de wèntí.

错了。因为九年级的第二天，我就认识「她」了。

dànshì wǒ cuòle. yīnwèi jiǔniánjí de dìèrtiān, wǒ jiù rènshi "tā" le.

Chapter Three

九年级 的 第二天，我 很 无聊。很多人都 跟 我 说，「你的 储物柜 里面 好不好看？」我 很 烦恼。我 不 知道 要 生 谁的 气，但是 我 很 生气。我 生气 因为 我 不 喜欢 他们 这麼 跟 我 说话。我 生气，因为 一个 好看 的 女孩子 看了 我 在 储物柜 里面。我 烦恼，因为 我 没有 再 看到 她 了。我 烦恼，因为 如果 我 看到 她，我 要 说 什麼？「谢谢 你 打开 我的 储物柜」？ 不好意思！

如果 我 不 矮…

第一节课 没有 什麼 特别 的。第一节 是 数学。我的 数学 不错。但是 我 不是 数学 高手。数学 高手（当然）就是 我的 哥哥。他的 数学 非常 好。因为 我们的 学校 不大，所以 老师 不多。有 两三个 数学 老师。他们 看到 我的 姓 的时候，他们 都 会 想到 我的 哥哥，所以 他们 以为 我的 数学 非常 好。两三个 星期 以後，他们 都 会 知道，我 不是 我的 哥哥。

我们 拿了 课本，写了 名字，点了 头。没 什麼 特别。英文课 和 科学课 也 没有 什麼 特别 的。

disānzhāng

jiǔniánjí de dìèrtiān, wǒ hěn wúliáo. hěnduō rén dōu gēnwǒ shuō, "nǐde chǔwùguì lǐmiàn hǎobùhǎokàn?" wǒ hěn fánnǎo. wǒ bù zhīdào yào shēng shéide qì, dànshì wǒ hěn shēngqì. wǒ shēngqì yīnwèi wǒ bù xǐhuān tāmen zhème gēn wǒ shuōhuà. wǒ shēngqì, yīnwèi yīge hǎokànde nǔháizǐ kànle wǒ zài chǔwùguì lǐmiàn. wǒ fánnǎo, yīnwèi wǒ méiyǒu zài kàndào tā le. wǒ fánnǎo, yīnwèi rúguǒ wǒ kàndào tā, wǒ yào shuō shénme? "xièxie nǐ dǎkāi wǒde chǔwùguì"? bùhǎoyìsi!

rúguǒ wǒ bù ǎi...

dìyījiékè méiyǒu shénme tèbié de. dìyījié shì shùxué. wǒde shùxué búcuò. dànshì wǒ búshì shùxué gāoshǒu. shùxué gāoshǒu (dāngrán) jiùshì wǒde gège. tāde shùxué fēicháng hǎo. yīnwèi wǒmen xuéxiào búdà, suǒyǐ lǎoshī bù duō. yǒu liǎngsānge shùxué lǎoshī. tāmen kàndào wǒde xìng deshíhòu, tāmen dōu huì xiǎngdào wǒde gège, suǒyǐ tāmen yǐwéi wǒde shùxué fēicháng hǎo. liǎngsānge xīngqī yǐhòu, tāmen dōu huì zhīdào, wǒ búshì wǒde gège.

wǒmen nále kèběn, xiěle míngzì, diǎnle tóu. méi shénme tèbié. yīngwén kè hé shùxuékè yě méiyǒu shénme tèbié de.

但是历史课就很特别!

不是老师很特别, 也不是课本很特别。就是坐在我前面的那位女孩子。

她的头髮很长。长长黑色的头髮, 很特别的头髮, 很美的头髮。我没有看她的脸以前, 已经喜欢她的头髮。但是她把课本给我的时候, 我才看了她的脸。就是打开了我储物柜的那个女孩子! 她的英文有一点特别, 因为她不是美国人。她是中国人! 我一看她, 就爱上了她。

我们的学校没有中国人。我们都是白人。黑人、西班牙侨, 我们都没有。我们都是白人。我也不是不喜欢我们学校的女孩子。我们学校的女孩子不是不好看, 但是这个中国女孩子就很特别。虽然她没有跟我说话, 但是我知道她很特别。

我不知道历史老师那天说了什麼话。我都在想「她」。她是哪里人? 她的家在哪儿? 我为什麼没有听说有新的学生? 还是我听说了, 但是我没有想她会这麼美、这麼特别?

我也不知道那个美女叫什麼名字, 但是我爱上了她。我为什麼没有听老师说

dànshì lìshǐ kè jiù hěn tèbié!

búshì lǎoshī hěn tèbié, yě búshì kèběn hěn tèbié. jiùshì zuò zài wǒ qiánmiàn de nàwèi nǚháizǐ.

tāde tóufa hěncháng. chángcháng hēisè de tóufǎ, hěn tèbié de tóufa. hěn měi de tóufa. wǒ méiyǒu kàn tāde liǎn yǐqián, yǐjīng xǐhuān tāde tóufa. dànshì tā bǎ kèběn gěi wǒ deshíhòu, wǒ cái kànle tāde liǎn. jiùshì dǎkāile wǒ chǔwùguì de nàge nǚháizǐ! tāde yīngwén yǒu yīdiǎn tèbié, yīnwèi tā búshì měiguórén. tā shì zhōngguórén! wǒ yīkàn tā, jiù àishàngle tā.

wǒmen de xuéxiào méiyǒu zhōngguórén. wǒmen dōu shì báirén. hēirén, xībānyáqiáo, wǒmen dōu méiyǒu. wǒmen dōu shì báirén. wǒ yě búshì bùxǐhuān wǒmen xuéxiào de nǚháizǐ. wǒmen xuéxiào de nǚháizǐ búshì bùhǎokàn, dànshì zhège zhōngguó nǚháizǐ jiù hěn tèbié. suīrán tā méiyǒu gēnwǒ shuōhuà, dànshì wǒ zhīdào tā hěn tèbié.

wǒ bùzhīdào lìshǐ lǎoshī nàtiān shuōle shénme huà.

wǒ dōu zài xiǎng "tā". tā shì nǎlǐ rén? tāde jiā zài nǎer? wǒ wèishénme méiyǒu tīngshuō yǒu

她的 名字? 我 都 在听: 老师 会不会 叫 她 的 名字? 但是 他 没有。 下课 的 时候, 我 还 不知道 我 爱上 的 女孩子 叫 什麼 名字。

但是 下课 的 时候, 我 也 就 知道, 我 知 不知道 她的 名字 都 没有关系。 因为 那个 很美的、 头髮 很长的、 坐 在 我 前面 的、 我 爱上 的 女孩子 很高。

没办法! 矮矮 的 我? 她 怎麼 会 喜欢 我? 我 太矮了。 但是 我 要 他 喜欢 我。 我 要 想办法。 但是 没办法。

但是, 虽然 没办法, 我 吃 中饭 的 时候, 我 都 在 想 她。 我 上 体育课 的 时候, 我 都 在 想 他。 回家 的 时候 我 也 想了 他。 给 牛 挤奶 的 时候, 给 猪 吃 东西 的 时候, 我 也 想 她。 功课 我 做得 不好, 因为 我 写了 两 三个 字 以後, 我 就会 想到 「她」。 没办 法。 但是 我 都 在 想。

我 不是 很 不好看 的 男孩子。 我 不是 很 笨的 人。 我的 衣服 不错。 一个 很美的、头 髮 很长的 女孩子 会 爱 我, 不是 吗? 但是 一个 很美的、 头髮 很长的、长得 很高的 女 孩子 呢? 不会! 没办法。

xīnde xuéshēng? háishì wǒ tīngshuōle, dànshì wǒ méiyǒu xiǎng tā huì zhème měi, zhème tèbié?

wǒ yě bù zhīdào nàge měinǚ jiào shénme míngzì, dànshì wǒ àishàngle tā. wǒ wèishénme méiyǒu tīng lǎoshī shuō tāde míngzì? wǒ dōu zàitīng: lǎoshī huìbúhuì jiào tāde míngzì? dànshì tā méiyǒu. xiàkè deshíhòu, wǒ hái bù zhīdào wǒ àishàngde nǚháizǐ jiào shénme míngzì.

dànshì xiàkè deshíhòu, wǒ yě jiù zhīdào, wǒ zhībùzhīdào tāde míngzì dōu méiyǒuguànxi. yīnwèi nàge hěnměide, tóufa hěnchángde, zuòzài wǒ qiánmiàn de, wǒ àishàng de nǚháizǐ hěn gāo.

méibànfǎ! ǎiǎi de wǒ? tā zěnme huì xǐhuān wǒ? wǒ tàiǎile. dànshì wǒ yào tā xǐhuān wǒ. wǒ yào xiǎng bànfǎ. dànshì méibànfǎ.

dànshì, suīrán méibànfǎ, wǒ chī zhōngfàn deshíhòu, wǒ dōu zài xiǎng tā. wǒ shàng tǐyùkè deshíhòu, wǒ dōu zài xiǎng tā. huíjiā deshíhòu wǒ yě xiǎngle tā. gěi niú jǐnǎi deshíhòu, gěi zhū chī dōngxī deshíhòu, wǒ yě xiǎng tā. gōngkè wǒ zuòde bùhǎo, yīnwèi wǒ xiěle liǎngsānge zì yǐhòu, wǒ jiùhuì xiǎngdào "tā". méibànfǎ. dànshì wǒ dōu zài xiǎng.

wǒ búshì hěn bùhǎokàn de nánháizǐ. wǒ búshì hěnbènde rén. wǒde yīfú búcuò. yīge hěnměide, tóufa hěnchángde nǚháizǐ huì ài wǒ, búshì ma? dànshì yīge hěnměide, tóufa hěnchángde, zhǎngde hěngāo de nǚháizǐ ne? búhuì! méibànfǎ.

Chapter Four

我怎麼让Julia喜欢我呢？

（「她」的名字叫Julia。我第二天就听老师说的。Ju-li-a。很好听，不是吗？）

这个问题，我想了很久。我上课的时候想。我在家的时候也想。但是，我都没办法。

到了星期五，我学了很多「Julia学」。我是「Julia高手」了。我知道她姓Lin。我知道她八月二十号到了美国。我知道她喜欢吃披萨，不喜欢吃汉堡包。她的眼睛咖啡色。她有很特别的味道。是香草的味道。不是！是肉桂的味道。也不是！是…是「她」的味道。那麼香！我很喜欢。我不知道是什麼味道，但是我很喜欢。我在历史课的时候，我很喜欢那个味道。我知道她有一个弟弟。我知道她的头髮多长。我知道她的爸爸还在中国。我知道很多。

但是我不知道怎麼让她喜欢我。

去年我不喜欢历史课。我们要看很多书。我虽然喜欢看书，但是我喜欢看的

dìsizhāng

wǒ zěnme ràng Julia xǐhuān wǒ ne?

("tā" de míngzǐ jiào Julia. wǒ dièrtiān jiù tīng lǎoshī suōde. ju-li-a! hěn hǎotīng, búshì ma?)

zhège wèntí, wǒ xiǎngle hěnjiǔ. wǒ shàngkè deshíhòu xiǎng. wǒ zàijiā deshíhòu wǒ yě xiǎng. dànshì, wǒ dōu méibànfǎ.

dàole xīngqī wǔ, wǒ xuéle hěnduō "Julia xué". wǒ shì "Julia gāoshǒu" le. wǒ zhīdào tā xìng lin. wǒ zhīdào tā bāyuè èrshí hào dàole měiguó. wǒ zhīdào tā xǐhuān chī pīsà, bù xǐhuān chī hànbǎobāo. tāde yǎnjīng kāfēisè. tā yǒu hěn tèbié de wèidào. shì xiāngcǎo de wèidào. búshì! shì ròuguì de wèidào. yě búshì! shì...shì "tā" de wèidào. nàme xiāng! wǒ hěn xǐhuān. wǒ bù zhīdào shì shénme wèidào, dànshì wǒ hěn xǐhuān. wǒ zài lìshǐkè deshíhòu, wǒ hěn xǐhuān nàge wèidào. wǒ zhīdào tā yǒu yīge dìdi. wǒ zhīdào tāde tóufa duōcháng. wǒ zhīdào tāde bàba hái zài zhōngguó. wǒ zhīdào hěnduō.

dànshì wǒ bù zhīdào zěnme ràng tā xǐhuān wǒ.

qùnián wǒ bù xǐhuān lìshǐkè. wǒmen yào kàn hěnduō shū. wǒ suīrán xǐhuān kànshū,

书（当然！）不是历史书。 但是今年，我很喜欢历史课了。 当然，那就是因为 Julia 坐在我前面。

有一天，我跟我哥哥说：「哥，你怎麽让 Lauren 喜欢你？」

Jared 笑了。「我怎麽让她喜欢我呢？她怎麽不喜欢我呢？我好看。 我踢橄榄球踢得很好。 我很高。 我有金色头髮。她当然喜欢我。」他看了看我。「为什麽？有一个男孩子要让 Lauren 喜欢他了吗？」

我没有看哥哥的眼睛。 我很不好意思。「不是。 我怎麽说？你们是…那是…没关係。 我不说了。」

Jared 看了看我。「你喜欢上一个女孩子，不是吗？」

我很快地说「不是！ 我没有！ 我…」

但是 Jared 在叫：「Josh 喜欢一个女孩子了！ Josh 喜欢一个女孩子了！」我的脸红了。 我很想打他，但是那个时候，妈妈就在那儿。

「你们说什麽？ Josh 有女朋友了吗？」

「我没有！ 没有！」

dànshì wǒ xǐhuān kàndeshū (dàngrán!) búshì lìshǐshū, dànshì jīnnián, wǒ hěn xǐhuān lìshǐkè le. dāngrán, nà jiùshì yīnwèi Julia zuòzài wǒ qiánmiàn.

yǒuyītiān, wǒ gēn wǒ gège shuō: "gè, nǐ zěnme ràng Lauren xǐhuān nǐ?"

Jared xiàole. "wǒ zěnme ràng tā xǐhuān wǒ ne? tā zěnme bù xǐhuān wǒ ne? wǒ hǎokàn. wǒ tī gǎnlǎnqiú tīde hěnhǎo. wǒ hěn gāo. wǒ yǒu jīnsè tóufa. tā dāngrán xǐhuān wǒ." tā kànlekàn wǒ. "wèishénme? yǒu yīge nánháizi yào ràng Lauren xǐhuān tā le ma?"

wǒ méiyǒu kàn gège de yǎnjīng. wǒ hěn bùhǎoyìsi. "búshì. wǒ zěnme shuō? nǐmen shì... nàshì...méiguānxi. wǒ bùshuō le."

Jared kànlekàn wǒ. "nǐ xǐhuān shàng yīge nǔháizǐ, búshì ma?"

wǒ hěnkuàide shuō "búshī! wǒ méiyǒu! wǒ..."

dànshì Jared zài jiào: "Josh xǐhuān yīge nǔháizǐ le! Josh xǐhuān yīge nǔháizǐ le!" wǒde liǎn hóngle. wǒ hěn xiǎng dǎtā, danshi nàge shíhòu, māma jiù zài nàr.

"nǐmen shuō shénme? Josh yǒu nǔpéngyǒu le ma?"

"wǒ méiyǒu! méiyǒu!"

妈妈看了看我，再看了 Jared。「Jared，你不是要去挤牛奶的吗？」

Jared 笑了。「都挤好了。」

「那麼，猪呢？」

「我已经…」

妈妈跟他说：「我想，你现在就要去看一看，它们都还好吗。」Jared 很不高兴，但是妈妈要他去，所以他就去了。

Jared 去了以後，妈妈就跟我说：「Josh，你不是有女朋友，就是喜欢上一个女孩子，不是吗？」我虽然没有说话，但是妈妈说：「所以，你喜欢上的那个女孩子，你要她喜欢你。我知道。但是你不高兴，因为你还很矮，不是吗？」

我看了看她。她怎麼知道这麼多？我什麼都没有跟他说。

「Josh，你要让她看你的特别。不是高不高，也不是踢不踢橄榄球。但是没有问题。」她笑了。「你已经很特别。」

特别。我有什麼特别？我不高。我不是很好看。我没有很多朋友。我的数学不好，英文不好，历史不好。西班牙语还好，但是…

māma kànlekàn wǒ, zài kànle Jared. "Jared, nǐ búshì yào qù jǐniúnǎi de ma?"

Jared xiàole. "dōu jǐhǎole."

"nàme, zhū ne?"

"wǒ yǐjīng..."

māma gēn tā shuō, "wǒ xiǎng, nǐ xiànzài jiùyào qù kànyīkàn, tāmen dōu háihǎo ma." Jared hěn bù gāoxìng, dànshì māma yào tā qù, suǒyǐ tā jiù qùle.

Jared qùle yǐhòu, māma jiù gēn wǒ shuō: "Josh, nǐ búshì yǒu nǚpéngyǒu, jiùshì xǐhuān shàng yīge nǚháizǐ, búshì ma?" wǒ suīrán méiyǒu shuōhuà, dànshì māma shuō: "suǒyǐ, nǐ xǐhuān shàng de nàge nǚháizǐ, nǐ yào tā xǐhuān nǐ. wǒ zhīdào. dànshì nǐ bù gāoxìng, yīnwèi nǐ hái hěn ǎi, búshì ma?"

wǒ kànlekàn tā. tā zěnme zhīdào zhème duō? wǒ shénme dōu méiyǒu gēntā shuō.

"Josh, nǐ yào ràng tā kàn nǐde tèbié. búshì gāobùgāo, yě búshì tī bùtī gǎnlǎnqiú. dànshì méiyǒuwèntí." tā xiàole. "nǐ yǐjīng hěn tèbié."

tèbié. wǒ yǒu shénme tèbié? wǒ bù gāo. wǒ búshì hěn hǎokàn. wǒ méiyǒu hěnduō péngyǒu. wǒde shùxué búhǎo, yīngwén bùhǎo, lìshǐ bùhǎo. xībānyáyǔ háihǎo, dànshì…

但是⋯

如果我会学好西班牙语，我也会学好中文！在我们的学校，没有一个会说中文的人！我如果会说中文，我就会独一无二了。Julia 是中国人。她会喜欢会说中文的我！

dànshì…

rúguǒ wǒ huì xuéhǎo xībānyáyǔ, wǒ yě huì xuéhǎo zhōngwén! zài wǒmen de xuéxiào, méiyǒu yīge huì shuō zhōngwén de rén! wǒ rúguǒ huì shuō zhōngwén, wǒ jiù huì dúyīwúèr le. Julia shì zhōngguórén. tā huì xǐhuān huì shuō zhōngwén de wǒ!

Chapter Five

　　要「特別」也好。问题是，我怎麼学好中文？我们的学校没有中文课。当然没有！如果学校有，学中文的同学就会很多。所以我很高兴。

　　但是如果学校没有，在哪儿有中文课？

　　星期六，我在我的卧室。我虽然有功课要做，但是我都在想那个「特别」的问题。在哪儿有中文课？我想了很久，然後我打开了我的电脑。

　　我现上了 Facebook。我看了我的 Facebook 朋友。他们不多。他们也都不会说中文。没办法。

　　我上了Google，打了「Chinese」。太多了！我想了想。我要打什麼字呢？我打了「Chinese lessons」。有网站！有很多网站！

　　我看了第一个网站。网站叫「RoseColored Rock」。那个网站很好看。有很多高兴的美国人。他们都学中文。他们用 CD 学中文。但是「RoseColored

dìwǔzhāng

yāo "tèbié" yěhǎo. wèntí shì, wǒ zěnme xuéhǎo zhōngwén? wǒmen de xuéxiào méiyǒu zhōngwénkè. dāngrán méiyǒu! rúguǒ xuéxiào yǒu, xué zhōngwén de tóngxué jiù huì hěnduō. suǒyǐ wǒ hěn gāoxìng.

dànshì rúguǒ xuéxiào méiyǒu, zài nǎer yǒu zhōngwénkè?

xīngqīliù, wǒ zài wǒde wòshì. wǒ suīrán yǒu gōngkè yàozuò, dànshì wǒ dōu zài xiǎng nàge "tèbié" de wèntí. zài nǎer yǒu zhōngwénkè? wǒ xiǎngle hěnjiǔ, ránhòu wǒ dǎkāile wǒde diànnǎo.

wǒ xiān shàngle facebook. wǒ kànle wǒde facebook péngyǒu. tāmen bùduō. tāmen yě dōu búhuì shuō zhōngwén. méibànfǎ.

wǒ shàngle google, dǎle "chinese". tàiduōle! wǒ xiǎnglexiǎng. wǒ yào dǎ shénme zì ne? wǒ dǎle "chinese lessons". yǒu wǎngzhàn! yǒu hěnduō wǎngzhàn!

wǒ kànle dìyīge wǎngzhàn. wǎngzhàn jiào "rosecolored rock". nàhe wǎngzhàn hěn hǎokàn. yǒu hěnduō gāoxìng de meǒguó rén. tāmen dōu xué zhōngwén. tāmen yòng CD xué

Rock」很贵！我说「很贵」吗？是「非常贵」。因为「RoseColored Rock」那麽贵，我想知道，人对「RoseColored Rock」有什麽意见？

我打了「RoseColored Rock opinions」。有很多！很多人都对「RoseColored Rock」有意见！我看了第一个意见。这个意见不在「RoseColored Rock」的网站上。意见是：「我买了 RoseColored Rock。RoseColored Rock 很不好。我不喜欢。」

第二个意见是一个学生的意见。她说：「我门的学校要我们用 RoseColored Rock。但是很无聊。我不喜欢用。虽然我喜欢中文，但是我不想用 RoseColored Rock 学。」

我看了网站。有一百三十七个意见。有一个人喜欢「RoseColored Rock」。有一百三十六个人说「RoseColored Rock」很无聊。我再看了喜欢「RoseColored Rock」那个人的姓名。对了！就是卖「RoseColored Rock」的一个人！当然他对「RoseColored Rock」的意见那麽好！

我没有很多钱。我也不喜欢无聊。所以我没有买「RoseColored Rock」。

zhōngwén. dànshì "rosecolored rock" hěnguì!
wǒ shuō "hěnguì" ma? wǒ shuō "hěnguì" ma?
shì "fēicháng guì". yīnwèi "rosecolored rock"
nàme guì, wǒ xiǎng zhīdào. rén duì "rosecolored
rock" yǒu shénme yìjiàn?

wǒ dǎle "rosecolored rock opinions". yǒu
hěnduō! hěnduō rén duì "rosecolored rock"
yǒu yìjiàn! wǒ kànle dìyīge yìjiàn. zhège
yìjiàn búzài "rosecolored rock" de wǎngzhàn
shàng. yìjiàn shì: "wǒ mǎile rosecolored rock.
rosecolored rock hěn bùhǎo. wǒ bù xǐhuān.

dièrge yìjiàn shì yīge xuéshēng de yìjiàn.
tā shuō: "wǒmen de xuéxiào yào wǒmen yòng
"rosecolored rock. dànshì hěn wúliáo. wǒ bù
xǐhuān yòng. suīrán wǒ xǐhuān zhōngwén,
dànshì wǒ bù xiǎng yòng rosecolored rock xué."

wǒ kànle wǎngzhàn. yǒu yībǎisānshíqī ge
yìjiàn. yǒu yīgè rén xǐhuān "rosecolored rockl".
yǒu yībǎisānshíliù ge rén shuō "rosecolored
rock" hěn wúliáo. wǒ zài kànle xǐhuān
"rosecolored rock" nàge rén de xìngmìng.
duìle! jiùshì mài "rosecolored rock" de yīge
rén! dāngrán tā duì "rosecolored rock" de yìjiàn
name hǎo!

wǒ méiyǒu hěnduō qián. wǒ yě bu xǐhuān
wúliáo. suǒyǐ wǒ méiyǒu mǎi "rosecolored

但是 我 还 要 学 好 中文。怎麼 办?

我 再 想 了 很 久。然後 我 打 了「Chinese language tutor」。有 很 多 网站。我 上 了 一 个。在 那 个 网站 上 有 很 多 中国人。他们 想 教 中文。很 多 都 会 说 英文。我 看 了 他 们。有 没有 一 个 独一无二 的 中文 老师?

我 看 到 了「Bubba 老师」的 时候,我 就 知道,他 很 特别。我 要 独一无二 的 中文 老师,Bubba老师 就 是 那个人!

Bubba老师 的 家 不 在 中国。他 的 家 在 巴西!中文 老师 怎麼 在 巴西?很 特别! Bubba老师 没有 头髮。他 的 眼睛 是 蓝色 的。他 会 说 西班牙文、法文、德文、俄 文、拉丁文、斯瓦希里语 和 冰岛语!但是 他 是 中国人。他 教中文。他 也 不 要 钱! 一 个 不 要 钱 的 中文 老师!他 用 Skype 上 课。

Bubba老师 独一无二!我 知道,Bubba老 师 就 是 我 要 的 中文 老师。

rock".

dànshì wǒ hái yáo xuéhǎo zhōngwén. zěnme bàn?

wǒ zài xiǎngle hěnjiǔ. ránhòu wǒ dǎle "chinese language tutor". yǒu hěnduō wǎngzhàn. wǒ shàngle yīge. zài nàge wǎngzhàn shàng yǒu hěnduō zhōngguórén. tāmen xiǎng jiào zhōngwén. hěnduō dōu huì shuō yīngwén. wǒ kànle tāmen. yǒuméiyǒu yīge dúyīwúèr de zhōngwén lǎoshī?

wǒ kàndàole "bubba lǎoshī" deshíhòu, wǒ jiù zhīdào, tā hěn tèbié. wǒ yào dúyīwúèr de zhōngwén lǎoshī, bubba lǎoshī jiù shì nàge rén!

bubba lǎoshī de jiā búzài zhōngguó. tāde jiā zài bāxī! zhōngwén lǎoshī zěnme zài bāxī? hěn tèbié! bubba lǎoshī méiyǒu tóufa. tāde yǎnjīng shì lánsè de. tā huìshuō xībānyáwén, fǎwén, déwén, èwén,lādīngwén, sīwǎxīlǐyǔ hé bīngdǎoyǔ! dànshì tā shì zhōngguórén. tā jiào zhōngwén. tā yě búyào qián! yīge búyàoqián de zhōngwén lǎoshī! tā yòng skype shàngkè.

bubba lǎoshī dúyīwúèr! wǒ zhīdào! bubba lǎoshī jiùshì wǒ yàode zhōngwén lǎoshī.

Chapter Six

Bubba 老师 没有 让 我 失望。

我 第二天 就 开始 上 他 的 课。谁 都 不 知道 我 开始 了。因为 Bubba 老师 不要 钱，我 不用 跟 我 父母 要 钱。这样 很 好。虽然 我 父母 对我 很好，但是 他们 都 会 问 很多 问题。因为 去年 的 台风，我们 现在 没有 很多 钱。我 知道 我 父母 都 很 紧张，因为 没有 钱。我 不想 让 他们 更 紧张 了。还有，如果 妈妈 问 我 为什么 要 学 中文，她 就 会 知道 Julia 的 事，而 那 就 会 很 麻烦 了。但是 更 麻烦 的 是，如果 妈妈 知道 我 在 学校 的 麻烦，她 会 想要 问 很多 问题。所以，我 不 要 爸爸 妈妈 知道 我 开始 学 中文 了!

因为 Bubba 老师 用 Skype 上课，所以 我 不用 出去。我 都 在 家 上课。因为 他 不要 钱，所以 没有 人 知道。对 别人 来说，我 还 是 不好看 的 Josh，不「独一无二」的 Josh，矮得 不可以 踢 橄榄球 的 Josh。虽然 我 不是 很喜欢 别人 那麼 想，但是 这样 比 让 他们 知道 好。

Bubba 老师 不错。我 第一天 就 很喜欢 他 了。他 说 的 中文 我 都 听得懂。我 特别 喜欢

dìliùzhāng

bubba lǎoshī méiyǒu ràng wǒ shīwàng.

wǒ dìèrtiān jiù kāishǐ shàng tāde kè. shéi dōu bùzhīdào wǒ kāishǐ le. yīnwèi bubba lǎoshī búyào qián, wǒ búyòng gēn wǒ fùmǔ yào qián. zhèyàng hěn hǎo. suīrán wǒ fùmǔ duìwǒ hěnhǎo, dànshì tāmen dōu huì wèn hěnduō wèntí. yīnwèi qùnián de táifēng, wǒmen xiànzài méiyǒu hěnduō qián. wǒ zhīdào wǒ fùmǔ dōu hěnjǐnzhāng, yīnwèi méiyǒu qián. wǒ bùxiǎng ràng tāmen gèngjǐnzhāng le. háiyǒu, rúguǒ māma wènwǒ wèishénme yàoxué zhōngwén, tā jiùhuì zhīdào Julia deshì. ér nàjiù huì hěn máfán le. dànshì gèngmáfánde shì, rúguǒ māma zhīdào wǒ zàixuéxiàode máfán, tā huì xiǎngyào wèn hěnduō wèntí. suǒyǐ, wǒ búyào bàbamāma zhīdào wǒ kāishǐ xuézhōngwén le!

yīnwèi bubba lǎoshī yòng skype shàngkè, suǒyǐ wǒ búyòng chūqù. wǒ dōu zài jiā shàngkè. yīnwèi tā búyào qián, suǒyǐ méiyǒu rén zhīdào. duì biérén láishuō, wǒ háishì bùhǎikàn de Josh, bù "dúyīwúèr" de Josh, ǎide bù kěyǐ tī gǎnlǎnqiú de Josh. suīrán wǒ búshì hěnxǐhuān biérén nàme xiǎng, dànshì zhèyàng bǐ ràng tāmen zhīdào hǎo.

bubba lǎoshī búcuò. wǒ dìyītiān jiù hěn xǐhuān tā le. tāshuōde zhōngwén wǒ dōu

的是，他都不给功课。在学校，功课很
多。我不想有更多的功课，所以 Bubba 的
课很不错。

　有一天，我跟 Bubba 老师上课的时候，
我哥哥就大声地叫我的名字。「Josh!
Josh!」我没有跟他说话。我忙。我在上
中文课。我怎麼要跟他说话？

　但是他再叫了一次。现在他的声音很
大了。「JOSH！！」

　我很快跟 Bubba 老师说了「不好意思」
，就把电脑关掉。我知道 Bubba 老师会
瞭解。十秒钟以後，我哥哥就在我的卧
室里面。

　「哥哥，你好。不好意思，我忘了我什
麼时候请了你到我的卧室来。」

　哥哥打了我的头。很痛！但是我都没
有说。

　「你为什麼都在卧室里面？你都在做
什麼？」

　「管你的事！」

　他又打了我。「管我的事吗？你就是
我的事。你是我的弟弟。很麻烦的弟弟，
但是没办法。」

tīngdedǒng. wǒ tèbié xǐhuānde shì, tādōu bùgěi gōngkè. zài xuéxiào, gōngkè hěnduō. wǒ bùxiǎng yǒu gèngduōde gōngkè. suǒyǐ bubba dekè hěnbúcuò.

yǒu yītiān, wǒ gēn bubba lǎoshī shàngkè deshíhòu, wǒ gēge jiù dàshēngde jiào wǒde míngzì. "Josh! Josh!" wǒ méiyǒu gēntā shuōhuà. wǒ máng. wǒ zài shàng zhōngwénkè. wǒ zěnme yào gēn tā shuōhuà?

dànshì tā zài jiàole yīcì. xiànzài tāde shēngyīn hěndà le. "Josh!"

wǒ hěnkuài gēn bubba lǎoshī shuōle "bùhǎoyìsi", jiù bǎ diànnǎo guāndiào. wǒ zhīdào bubba lǎoshī huì liǎojiě. shímiǎozhōng yǐhòu, wǒ gēge jiù zài wǒde wòshì lǐmiàn.

"gēge, nǐ hǎo. bùhǎoyìsi! wǒ wàngle wǒ shénmeshíhòu qǐngle nǐ dào wǒde wòshì lái."

gegè dǎle wǒdetóu. hěntòng! dànshì wǒ dōu méiyǒu shuō.

"nǐ wèishénme dōu zài wòshì lǐmiàn? nǐ dōu zài zuò shénme?"

"guǎn nǐ deshì!"

tā yòu dǎle wǒ. "guǎnwǒdeshì ma? nǐ jiùshì wǒdeshì. nǐ shì wǒ de dìdi. hěn máfánde dìdi, dànshì méibànfǎ."

他看了我一眼。「听说你在学校有麻烦，是不是？」

我没有看他，也没有说话。我不好意思跟他说。Jared 在学校都没有问题。我怎麽跟他说，都是因为我太小了？

「我知道你在学校有麻烦。但是，我是高四学生了。你是高一。我没办法都跟你去上课。」

「我没有要你跟我去上课！」

「我知道。但是你一个人…听说 Billy Heller 要给你麻烦了。」

我很不高兴。Billy 是我们学校最大的、最不好的、最会给我麻烦的一个人。他是高一的同学，但是他很大。没有人喜欢他。他爸爸妈妈不喜欢他！他为什麽要管我的事？

哥哥看了我。「所以，因为 Billy Heller 要给你麻烦，我们要想办法。你有办法吗？」

「我有什麽办法呢？没办法。我死定了。」

哥哥笑了。「不一定。你知道，踢橄榄球的人都是高四的同学。但是今年我

tā kànle wǒ yīyǎn. tīngshuō nǐ zài xuéxiào yǒu máfán, shìbúshì?"

wǒ méiyǒu kàntā, yě méiyǒu shuōhuà. wǒ bùhǎoyìsi gēn tā shuō. Jared zài xuéxiào dōu méiyǒu wèntí. wǒ zěnme gēn tā shuō, dōu shì yīnwèi wǒ tàixiǎole?

"wǒ zhīdào nǐ zài xuéxiào yǒu máfán. dànshì, wǒ shì gāosì xuéshēng le. nǐ shì gāoyī. wǒ méibànfǎ dōu gēnnǐ qù shàngkè."

"wǒ méiyǒu yào nǐ gēnwǒ qù shàngkè!"

"wǒ zhīdào. danìshì nǐ yīgerén...tīngshuō Billy Heller yào gěi nǐ máfán le."

wǒ hěn bù gāoxìng. Billy shì wǒmen xuéxiào zuì dàde, zuì bùhǎode, zuì huì gěi wǒ máfán de yīge rén. tā shì gāoyī de tóngxué, dànshì tā hěn dà. méiyǒu rén xǐhuān tā. tā bàba māma bù xǐhuān tā! tā wèishénme yào guǎnwǒdeshì?

gege kànle wǒ. "suǒyǐ, yīnwèi Billy Heller yào gěinǐ máfán, wǒmen yào xiǎng bànfǎ. nǐ yǒu bànfǎ ma?"

"wǒ yǒu shénme bànfǎ ne? méi bànfǎ. wǒ sǐdìng le."

gège xiàole. "bù yídìng. nǐ zhīdào, tī zǔqiú de rén dōushì gāosì de tóngxué. dànshì jīnnián

们有一个，不是高四的。他是高一的同学！他踢橄榄球踢得非常好，但是他都没有朋友。你没有大的人，他没有朋友。所以，他就是你最好的朋友了！」

wǒmen yǒu yīge, búshì gāosì de. tā shì gāoyī de tóngxué. tā tī gǎnlǎnqiú tīde fēicháng hǎo, dànshì tā dōu méiyǒu péngyǒu. nǐ méiyǒu dàde rén, tā méiyǒu péngyǒu. suǒyǐ, tā jiùshì nǐ zuìhǎode péngyǒu le!"

Chapter Seven

虽然我本来以为我不会喜欢 Christian，三个星期以後，我很喜欢他了。他是一个很好的朋友。最好的是，Billy Heller 知道 Christian 是我的朋友以後，他都不跟我说话了。他都不看我了！我很高兴。

我知道，我们是很奇怪的朋友。他很高，我不高。虽然我的朋友不多，但是我有朋友；Christian 一个朋友都没有。我很会说话，但是 Christian 都不喜欢说话。他真的都不说话。有的时候，我们在图书馆做功课的时候，我要看他还在不在，因为他两三个小时都不说话。

虽然 Christian 跟我是好朋友，但是我没有跟他说我学中文，也没有跟他说我喜欢 Julia。Christian 的历史老师是 Mr. Sanders；我的是 Mr. Golden。所以 Christian 没有看我在历史课看 Julia。虽然我们是好朋友，但是我不好意思。我不想跟他说。

有一个星期三，我们在图书馆做数学课的功课。我们的数学课老师太喜欢功

dìqīzhāng

suīrán wǒ běnlái yǐwéi wǒ búhuì xǐhuān Christian, sānge xīngqī yǐhòu, wǒ hěn xǐhuān tā le. tā shì yīge hěnhǎo de péngyǒu. zuìhǎode shì, Billy Heller zhīdào Christian shì wǒde péngyǒu yǐhòu, tā dōu bù gēn wǒ shuōhuà le. tā dōu búkàn wǒ le! wǒ hěn gāoxìng.

wǒ zhīdào, wǒmen shì hěn qíguài de péngyǒu. tā hěn gāo, wǒ bù gāo. suīrán wǒde péngyǒu bùduō, dànshì wǒ yǒu péngyǒu; Christian yīge péngyǒu dōu méiyǒu. wǒ hěnhuì shuōhuà, dànshì Christian dōu bù xǐhuān shuōhuà. tā zhēnde dōu bù shuōhuà. yǒudeshíhòu, wǒmen zài túshūguǎn zuò gōngkè deshíhòu wǒ yào kàn tā hái zàibúzài, yīnwèi tā liǎngsānge xiǎoshí dōu bù shuōhuà.

suīrán Christian gēn wǒ shì hǎo péngyǒu, dànshì wǒ méiyǒu gēn tā shuō wǒ xué zhōngwén, yě méiyǒu gēn tā shuō wǒ xǐhuān Julia. Christian de lìshǐ lǎoshī shì mr. sanders; wǒde shì mr. golden. suǒyǐ Christian méiyǒu kàn wǒ zài lìshǐkè kàn Julia. suīrán wǒmen shì hǎo péngyǒu, dànshì wǒ hěn bùhǎoyìsi. wǒ bùxiǎng gēn tā shuō.

yǒu yīge xīngqīsān, wǒmen zài túshūguǎn zuò shùxué kè de gōngkè. wǒmen de shùxuékè lǎoshī tài xǐhuān gōngkè. yīnwèi wǒmen dìèrtiān jiùyào

课。因为我们第二天就要考试了，所以我没有看 Christian，也没有跟他说话。

「Josh？」

他怎麽了？

「Josh？」 Christian 不在看数学书。我烦恼了。

「我们要考试！你为什麽不看数学书？」

Christian 没有说话了。但是我看了他的时候，他的脸很红。他为什麽脸红了？数学没有什么不好意思的。Christian 都不会脸红。他怎麽了？

「Christian？」他什么话都没有说。「你还好吗？」

他漫漫地看了我。「Christian，你怎麽了？我们要考试！」他要哭吗？

「我…我…」他的脸很红。他怎麽了？

「是那个女孩子。」我看了他。什么女孩子？ Christian 都想踢橄榄球。他不想女孩子。

「什么女孩子？」

「那个好看的。」

kǎoshì le, suǒyǐ wǒ méiyǒu kàn Christian, yě méiyǒu gēntā shuōhuà.

"Josh?"

tā zěnme le?

"Josh!" Christian bù zài kàn shùxuéshū. wǒ fánnǎo le.

"wǒmen yào kǎoshì! nǐ wèishénme bú kàn shùxuéshū?"

Christian méiyǒu shuōhuà le. dànshì wǒ kànle tā deshíhòu, tāde liǎn hěnhóng. tā wèishénme liǎnhóngle? shùxué méiyǒu shénme bùhǎoyìsi de. Christian dōu búhuì liǎnhóng. tā zěnme le?

"Christian?" tā shénme dōu méiyǒu shuō. nǐ háihǎo ma?

tā mànmānde kànle wǒ. "Christian, nǐ zěnme le? wǒmen yào kǎoshì!" tā yào kū ma?

"wǒ...wǒ..." tāde liǎn hěnhóng. tā zěnme le?

"shì nàge nǚháizǐ." wǒ kànle tā. shénme nǚháizǐ? Christian dōu xiǎng tī gǎnlǎnqiú. tā bùxiǎng nǚháizǐ.

"shénme nǚháizǐ?"

"nàge hǎokànde."

好了，是一个女孩子。一个好看的女孩子。她打了 Christian 吗？她喜欢 Christian？

「那个好看的女孩子怎麼了？」

Christian 没有看我。他不好意思地说，「我…很喜欢她。」

我想了想。我们学校没有很多很好看的女孩子。数学课没有好看的女孩子。英文课也没有。我想到了！在 Christian 的历史课有一个很好看的女孩子。她叫什么？ Sarah？ Sandra？ 最好不要说她的名字。我不要说错。

「喜欢一个女孩子不是问题。你请她看电影，就好了。」

Christian 不高兴。「不行。」

「看电影不行吗？请她吃饭。请她一」我也不知道要说什么了，因为在我们那儿不是看电影就是吃饭。没有第三个。

Christian 看了我。「不是看电影的问题，也不是吃饭的问题。问题是，我不可以请她。她很好看！你看我！我没有一」

Christian 苯吗？「没有什么？你很高。

hǎole, shì yīge nǚháizǐ. yīge hěnhǎokàn
de nǚháizǐ. tā dǎle Christian ma? tā xǐhuān
Christian?

"nàge hǎokànde nǚháizǐ zěnme le?"

Christian méiyǒu kàn wǒ. tā bùhǎoyìsi de
shuō, "wǒ... xǐhuān tā."

wǒ xiǎnglexiǎng. wǒmen xuéxiào méiyǒu
hěnduō hěn hǎokànde nǚháizǐ. shùxuékè méiyǒu
hǎokànde nǚháizǐ. yīngwénkè yě méiyǒu. wǒ
xiǎngdàole! zài Christian de lìshǐkè yǒu yīge
hěnhǎokàn de nǚháizǐ. tā jiào shénme? sarah?
sandra? zuìhǎo búyào shuō tāde míngzì. wǒ
búyào shuōcuò.

"xǐhuān yīge nǚháizǐ búshì wèntí. nǐ qǐng tā
kàn diànyǐng, jiù hǎole."

Christian bù gāoxìng. "bùxíng."

"kàn diànyǐng bùxíng ma? qǐng tā chīfàn.
qǐng tā—" wǒ yě bù zhīdào yào shuō shénme le,
yīnwèi zài wǒmen nàr búshì kàndiànyǐng jiùshì
chīfàn. méiyǒu dìsānge.

Christian kànle wǒ. "búshì kàndiànyǐng de
wèntí, yě búshì chīfàn de wèntí. wèntí shì,

wǒ bù kěyǐ qǐng tā. tā hěn hǎokàn! nǐ kàn
wǒ! wǒ méiyǒu —"

Christian bèn ma? "méiyǒu shénme? nǐ hěn

你打橄榄球。女孩子都喜欢高的男孩子。她们很喜欢打橄榄球的男孩子。你都没有问题!」

他生气地看了我。「没有问题吗?你是没有问题的人。 我不是!你的朋友很多,你的哥哥踢橄榄球,你在这儿很多年。但是我…我是新的。她不会喜欢我。」

「我没有问题吗?我?」

「对了。你很会说话。你都会跟女孩子说话。你知道女孩子喜欢什么。她们喜欢跟你说话。」

「但是——」我不知道我要说什么。

「Josh,你要帮忙。你可以帮我的忙吗?我很喜欢这个好看的女孩子,但是我不——我没有——我很想跟她说话,但是我都不会。你很会说话。你帮我说话,好不好?」

「可以,可以,但是你也可以…你给她写信,好不好?」

「你明天可以看一看吗?」

「好了,好了。我明天就看你写的信。但是现在我们要看数学,好不好?」

gāo. nǐ dǎ gǎnlǎnqiú. nǚháizǐ dōu xǐhuān gāode nánháizǐ. tāmen hěn xǐhuān dā gǎnlǎnqiú de nánháizǐ. nǐ dōu méiyǒu wèntí!"

tā shēngqìde kànle wǒ. "méiyǒuwèntí ma? nǐ shì méiyǒu wèntí de rén. wǒ búshì! nǐde péngyǒu yě hěnduō, nǐ de gège tīgǎnlǎnqiú, nǐ zài zhèr hěnduō nián. dànshì wǒ...wǒ shì xīnde. tā búhuì xǐhuān wǒ."

"wǒ méiyǒuwèntí ma? wǒ--"

"duìle. nǐ hěnhuì shuōhuà. nǐ dōu huì gēn nǚháizǐ shuōhuà. nǐ zhīdào nǚháizǐ xǐhuān shénme. tāmen xǐhuān gēn nǐ shuōhuà."

"dànshì—" wǒ bù zhīdào wǒ yào shuō shénme.

"Josh, nǐ yào bāngmáng. nǐ kěyǐ bāng wǒde máng ma? wǒ hěn xǐhuān zhèige hěnhǎokàn de nǚháizi, dànshì wǒ bù – wǒ méiyǒu – wǒ hěnxiǎng gēntā shuōhuà, dànshì wǒ dōu búhuì. nǐ hěnhuì shuōhuà. nǐ bāng wǒ shuōhuà, hǎobùhǎo?"

"kěyǐ, kěyǐ, dànshì nǐ yě kěyǐ...nǐ gěitā xiěxìn, hǎobùhǎo?"

"nǐ míngtiān kěyǐ kànyīkàn ma?"

"hǎole, hǎole. wǒ míngtiān jiù kàn nǐ xiěde xìn. dànshì xiànzài wǒmen yào kàn shùxué,

Christian 笑了。「好。」我们不说话了。

hǎobùhǎo?"

Christian xiàole. "hǎo." wǒmen bù shuōhuà le.

Chapter Eight

　　第二天，我七点十五分就在学校。我要看 Christian 写的信。

　　他的信是很－－很－－怎麼说呢？

　　很笨。

　　但是，我怎麼跟他说呢？

　　「Christian，虽然你说她很好看，但是你不要写"好看的女孩子：你好。"」

　　Christian 脸红了。「都是因为我不知道怎麼开始。开始很难。」

　　我多看了一点。「我想你很很很好看。我很喜欢你。」没办法！苯，苯，苯！

　　「"你是辣妹"？不行！你要说…」他要写什么？

　　Christian 跟我说，「就是。我不知道要跟她说什么，也不知道要给她写什么。太难了！」

　　「女人都难。」

　　Christian 没有听我说话。「你很会说

dìbāzhāng

dìèrtiān, wǒ qīdiǎn shíwùfēn jiù zài xuéxiào. wǒ yào kàn Christian xiěde xìn.

tāde xìn shì hěn...hěn...zěnme shuō ne? hěnbèn.

dànshì, wǒ zěnme gēn tā shuō ne?

"Christian, suīrán nǐ shuō tā hěnhǎokàn, dànshì nǐ búyào xiě 'hǎokàn de nǚháizǐ: nǐ hǎo.'"

Christian liǎnhóngle. "dōu shì yīnwèi wǒ bùzhīdào zěnme kāishǐ. kāishǐ hěnnán."

wǒ duō kànle yīdiǎn. "wǒ xiǎng nǐ hěnhěnhěn hǎokàn. wǒ hěn xǐhuān nǐ." méibànfǎ! bèn, bèn, bèn!

" 'nǐ shì làmèi'? bùxíng! nǐ yào shuō..." tā yào xiě shěnme?

Christian gēn wǒ shuō: "jiùshì. wǒ bù zhīdào yào gēn tā shuō shénme, yě bù zhīdào yào gěi tā xiě shénme. tàinánle!"

"nǚrén dōu nán."

Christian méiyǒu tīng wǒ shuōhuà. "nǐ

话，也很会写。不知道…你会不会…可不可以拜託你--」

「不行！你喜欢她。我不喜欢她。我怎麼写信给我不喜欢的女孩子？不行！」

Christian 跟我说：「拜託！我没有办法。我不会写！拜託！我很喜欢她。我太喜欢她。你说了你会帮忙，不是吗？」

我没办法。对了，我跟他说了。所以我要帮忙。「好了，好了。我帮你写。」

「太好了！你是很好的朋友。如果你给我写信，Julia 一定会喜欢我了！」

Julia? 我们学校有几个 Julia? 他喜欢的女孩子就是我的 Julia 吗?!?

在我们学校的女孩子很多。好看的女孩子也很多。叫 Julia 的女孩子很少。只有一个。为什麼 Christian 喜欢了我喜欢的女孩子？我的 Julia?

Julia 没有打开 Christian 的储物柜。学中文的人是我，不是 Christian。Christian 为什麼喜欢了 Julia?

Christian 看了看我。「你怎麼了？」

hěnhuì shuōhuà! yě hěnhuì xiě. bùzhīdào...nǐ
huìbúhuì...

kěbùkěyǐ bàituō nǐ..."

"bùxíng! nǐ xǐhuān tā. wǒ bù xǐhuān tā.
wǒ zěnme xiěxìn gěi wǒ bùxǐhuānde nǚháizǐ?
bùxíng!"

Christian gēn wǒ shuō: " bàituō! wǒ méiyǒu
bànfǎ. wǒ búhuì xiě! bàituō! wǒ hěn xǐhuān tā.
wǒ tài xǐhuān tā. nǐ shuōle nǐ huì bāngmáng,
búshì ma?"

wǒ méibànfǎ. duìle! wǒ gēn tā shuō le. suǒyǐ
wǒ yào bāngmáng. "hǎole, hǎole. wǒ bāng nǐ
xiě."

"tàihǎole! nǐ shì hěnhǎo de péngyǒu. rúguǒ
nǐ gěiwǒ xiěxìn, Julia yídìng huì xǐhuān wǒ le!"

Julia? wǒmen xuéxiào yǒu jǐge Julia? tā
xǐhuānde nǚháizǐ jiùshì wǒde Julia ma?!?

zài wǒmen xuéxiào de nǚháizǐ hěnduō.
hǎokàn de nǚháizǐ yě hěnduō. jiào Julia de
nǚháizǐ hěnshǎo. zhǐ yǒu yīge. wèishénme
Christian xǐhuān le wǒ xǐhuān de nǚháizǐ? wǒde
Julia?

Julia méiyǒu dǎkāi Christian de chǔwùguì.
xué zhóngwénde rén shì wǒ, búshì Christian.
Christian wéishénme xǐhuānle Julia?

Christian kànlekàn wǒ. "nǐ zěnme le?"

我很快地说：「没什么。我们看数学，好不好？」

虽然我看了我的数学书，但是我都不知道我看的是数学还是西班牙文。我什么都没有看懂。我都在想我的问题。我都不想数学考试了。

五点钟了。Christian 跟我说，「五点了。我回家了。你还要在这儿看书吗？」

我没有说话。Christian 看了看我。「你怎麼了？」

我没有看他。「没什么。我很快就回家去了。」

「好了。明天见！」

wǒ hěnkuàide shuō: "méi shénme. wǒmen kàn shùxué, hǎobùhǎo?"

suīrán wǒ kànle wǒde shùxuéshū, dànshì wǒ dōu bùzhīdào wǒ kànde shì shùxué háishì xībānyáwén. wǒ shénme dōu méiyǒu kàndǒng. wǒ dōu zài xiǎng wǒde wèntí. wǒ dōu bù xiǎng shùxué kǎoshì le.

wǔdiǎnzhōng lē. Christian gēn wǒ shuō, "wǔdiǎn le. wǒ huíjiā le. nǐ háiyào zài zhèr kànshū ma?"

wǒ méiyǒu shuōhuà. Christian kànlekàn wǒ. "nǐ zěnme le?"

wǒ méiyǒu kàntā. "méi shénme. wǒ hěnkuài jiù huíjiā qù le."

"hǎole. míngtiān jiān!"

Chapter Nine

在家，我想了 Christian 的问题。我跟他说了我要帮他忙。我不可以不帮他忙了，但是我很不高兴。我不想帮他忙。我喜欢 Julia！

Christian 好看。Christian 踢橄榄球。Christian 高！虽然他不会跟女孩子说话，但是如果我帮 Christian 写信，Julia 一定会喜欢他。

没有办法。Christian 是我哥哥的好朋友，也是我的朋友。他帮了我很大的忙。Billy Heller 不是麻烦了，都是因为 Christian 的帮忙。

我说了我要帮他忙，所以我要帮忙。

我们吃了晚饭以後，我就回我的房间。我跟 Christian 说我要帮忙，但是说话不够。我要写信。我要给 Julia 写信。虽然我很想要给她写信，跟她说我很喜欢她，但是我想写我的名字！我不想写 Christian 的名字。但是没有办法。我是他的朋友，所以我要帮忙。

我想了很久。Julia 会喜欢什么？我 --

dìjiǔzhāng

zàijiā, wǒ xiǎngle Christian de wèntí. wǒ gēntā shuōle wǒ yào bāng tā máng. wǒ bù kěyǐ bù bāng tā máng le, dànshì wǒ hěn bù gāoxìng. wǒ bùxiǎng bāng tā máng. wǒ xǐhuān Julia!

Christian hǎokàn. Christian tī gǎnlǎnqiú. Christian gāo! suīrán tā búhuì gēn nǚháizǐ shuōhuà, dànshì rúguǒ wǒ bāng Christian xiěxìn, Julia yídìng huì xǐhuān tā.

méiyǒu bànfǎ. Christian shì wǒ gège de hǎo péngyǒu, yě shì wǒ de péngyǒu. tā bāngle wǒ hěndàde máng. Billy Heller búshì máfán le, dōushì yīnwèi Christian de bāngmáng.

wǒ shuōle wǒ yào bāng tā máng, suǒyǐ wǒ yào bāngmáng.

wǒmen chīle wǎnfàn yǐhòu, wǒ jiù huí wǒde fángjiān. wǒ gēn Christian shuō wǒ yào bāng tā máng, dànshì shuōhuà búgòu. wǒ yào xiěxìn. wǒ yào gěi Julia xiěxìn. suīrán wǒ hěn xiǎngyào gěi tā xiěxìn, gēntāshuō wǒ hěn xǐhuān tā, dànshì wǒ xiǎng xiě wǒde míngzì! wǒ bùxiǎng xiě Christian de míngzì. dànshì méiyǒubànfǎ. wǒ shì tā de péngyǒu, suǒyǐ wǒ yào bāngmáng.

wǒ xiǎngle hěnjiǔ. Julia huì xǐhuān shénme?

我是说，Christian — 要 怎麼 跟她说 他 喜欢 她？

我 想了 Julia。 我 为什麼 喜欢 她？ 长头髮。 很美的 头髮。但是 我 不可以 写「我 喜欢 你的 头髮」。 很笨！ 那 是 Christian 写的信！ 我 要 写 独一无二 的 信， 很好 的 信， 因为 Julia 是 独一无二 的 女孩子。

八点了。 我 八点半 就要上 Bubba 老师 的 中文课 了。 对了！ Bubba 老师 会 知道。 他 会 跟我说 我 要 写 什么。

Bubba 老师 没有 让我 失望。 他 跟我说了 很多 很好听 的 中文。 都是 女孩子 会 喜欢 的。 虽然 我 要 写 英文 的 信 （因为 Christian 不会 说 中文） 但是 Bubba 老师 帮了 我 很大 的 忙。

下课 以後， 我 写了 五封信。 我 写得 很 快， 因为 我 都 知道 我 要 写 什么。 我 写的 时候， 我 都 在 想 Julia。 我 写了 我 要 写 的 信。 但是 名字 是 Christian 的 名字。

第二天， 我 在 学校 看到了 Christian。

「写好了吗？」

我 看了 我 手中的 信。 写好了。 写得 很

wǒ...wǒ shì shuō, Christian...yào zěnme gēn tā shuō tā xǐhuān tā?

wǒ xiǎngle Julia. wǒ wèishénme xǐhuān tā? chángtóufa. hěn měi de tóufa. dànshì wǒ bù kěyǐ xiě 'wǒ xǐhuān nǐde tóufa.' hěnbèn! nà shì Christian xiěde xìn! wǒ yào xiě dúyīwúèr de xìn, hěnhào de xìn, yīnwèi Julia shì dúyīwúèr de nǚháizǐ

bādiǎnle. wǒ bādiǎnbàn jiùyào shàng bubba lǎoshī de zhōngwénkè le. duìle! bubba lǎoshī huì zhīdào. tā huì gēnwǒshuō wǒ yào xiě shénme.

bubba lǎoshī méiyǒu ràng wǒ shīwàng. tā gēnwǒshuōle hěnduō hěnhǎotīng de zhōngwén. dōu shì nǚhàizǐ huì xǐhuān de. suīrán wǒ yào xiě yīngwén de xìn (yīnwèi Christian búhuì shuō zhōngwén) dànshì bubba lǎoshī bāngle wǒ hěndàde máng.

xiàkè yǐhòu, wǒ xiěle wǔfēngxìn. wǒ xiěde hěnkuài, yīnwèi wǒ dōu zhīdào wǒ yào xiě shénme. wǒ xiě deshíhòu, wǒ dōu zài xiǎng Julia. wǒ xiěle wǒ yào xiěde xìn. dànshì míngzì shì Christian de míngzì.

dìèrtiān, wǒ zài xuéxiào kàndàole Christian.

"xiěhàole ma?"

wǒ kànle wǒ shǒuzhōngde xìn. xiěhàole. xiěde hěnhǎo! wǒ bùxiǎng gěi Christian wǒ

好！我不想给Christian我写的信。但是，没办法。

我想了一分钟。「你什麼时候会看到她？」

Christian 说：「我不知道。我把信放在她的储物柜里面，好不好？」

「把信放在储物柜里面吗？你不想把信给她吗？你不要看她看信吗？」

「我…我…」

「你知道，如果她喜欢你，你要跟她说话！」

「我知道。但是不是今天。今天我要把信放在她的储物柜里面。她不在的时候，我就把信放在里面。」

「好了，好了。」我把五封信都给Christian。

他看了看信，就把五封信都放在他的数学书里面。

「太好了！谢谢你！谢谢！Julia 看了这些信以後，一定会喜欢我！」

我没有看 Christian。「对了。我知道，Julia 一定会喜欢你。」还好我们要去考

xiěde xìn. dànshì, méibànfǎ.

wǒ xiǎngle yīfēnzhōng. "nǐ shénmeshíhòu huì kàndào tā?"

Christian shuō: "wǒ bù zhīdào. wǒ bǎ xìn fàngzài tāde chǔwùguì lǐiàn, hǎobùhǎo?"

"bǎ xìn fàngzài tāde chǔwùguì lǐiàn ma? nǐ bùxiǎng bǎ xìn gěitā ma? nǐ búyào kàn tā kànxìn ma?"

"wǒ...wǒ..."

"nǐ zhīdào, rúguǒ nǐ xǐhuān tā, nǐ yào gēntā shuōhuà!"

"wǒ zhīdào. dànshì búshì jīntiān. jīntiān wǒ yào bǎ xìn fàngzài tāde chǔwùguì lǐiàn. tā búzài deshíhòu, wǒ jiù bǎ xìn fàngzài lǐmiàn."

"hǎole, "hǎole." wǒ bǎ wǔfēngxìn dōu gěi Christian.

tā kànlekàn xìn, jiù bǎ wǔfēngxìn dōu fàngzài tāde shùxuéshū lǐmiàn.

"tàihǎole! xièxiè nǐ! xièxiè! Julia kànle zhèxiē xìn yǐhòu, yídìng huì xǐhuān wǒ!"

wǒ méiyǒu kàn Christian. "duìle. wǒ zhīdào, Julia yídìng huì xǐhuān nǐ." háihǎo wǒmen yào qù kǎoshì. wǒ bù xiǎng gēn Christian shuōhuà

试。 我 不 想 跟 Christian 说话 了。 我 快要 哭 了。 但是， 男孩子 不哭， 对不对？

天气 冷了。 我 感冒了。 我 喷嚏 很多。 什么 都 很 麻烦。 但是 我 不是 因为 天气 不好， 还是 身体 不好， 而 不高兴。

我 不高兴 因为 我 写信 写的 很好。

但是， 我 说得 不对。 不是「我」写信， 而是「他」写信。 那些 信 都是「Christian 写的 信」， 而 不是「Josh 写的 信」。 我 每天 都 要 看 Julia 看「Christian 写的 信」。

「你看！」 Julia 笑着 跟 她的 朋友们 说。「Christian 都 不说话， 但是 他 很会 写信！ 他 很 喜欢 我！ 我 很 想 跟他 说话！」

我 不小心地 喷嚏 了。 Julia 跟 她的 朋友 看了看 我。 我 跟 她们 说：「不好意思」。

我 听得 很不 高兴， 因为 Julia 都 看得 很 高兴。我 越看 Julia 看「Christian」的信， 我 越 不高兴， 但是 没办法。 我 不可以 跟 Julia 说， 她 喜欢 看的信 都 是 我 写的。

我 功课 做得 不好了。 我 考试 考得 不好。 但是 我 很难 想 数学 和 英文课。 我 都 要 想办法， 但是 没办法。

le. wǒ kuàiyào kūle. dànshì, nánháizǐ bùkū, duìbúduì?

tiānqì lěngle. wǒ gǎnmàole. wǒ pēntì hěnduō. shénme dōu hěn máfán. dànshì wǒ búshì yīnwèi tiānqì bùhǎo, háishì shēntǐ bùhǎo, ér bù gāoxìng.

wǒ bùgāoxìng yīnwèi wǒ xiěxìn xiěde hěnhǎo.

dànshì, wǒ shuōde búduì. búshì "wǒ" xiěxìn, érshì "tā" xiěxìn. nàxiē xìn dōu shì "Christian xiěde xìn", érbúshì "Josh xiědexìn". wǒ měitiān dōu yào kàn Julia kàn "Christian xiěde xìn".

"nǐ kàn!" Julia xiàozhe gēn tāde péngyǒumen shuō. Christian dōu bùshuōhuà, dànshì tā hěnhuì xiěxìn! tā hěn xǐhuān wǒ! wǒ hěn xiǎng gēntā shuōhuà!"

wǒ bùxiǎoxīnde pēntì le. Julia gēn tāde péngyǒu kànlekàn wǒ. wǒ gēn tāmen shuō: bùhǎoyìsī. wǒ tīngde hěn bù gāoxìng, yīnwèi Julia dōu kànde hěn gāoxìng. wǒ yuèkàn Julia kàn "Christian" de xìn, wǒ yuè bù gāoxìng, dànshì méibànfǎ. wǒ bù kěyǐ gēn Julia shuō, tā xǐhuān kàndexìn dōu shì wǒ xiěde.

wǒ gōngkè zuòde bùhǎo le, wǒ kǎoshì kǎode bùhǎo. dànshì wǒ hěnnán xiǎng shùxué hé yīngwénkè. wǒ dōu yào xiǎng bànfǎ. dànshì méibànfǎ.

Julia 喜欢的话 都是 我的话。 但是 Julia 喜欢的 人 不是 我，而是 Christian。

真糟糕！

Julia xǐhuāndehuà dōushì wǒdehuà. dànshì Julia xǐhuānde rén búshì wǒ, érshì Christian.

zhēnzāogāo!

Chapter Ten

一个 星期四， 我 在 学校 餐厅 的时候，就 听到了 Christian。 他 在 叫 我的 名字。「Josh！ Josh！ 」

糟糕。 他 是不是 要 跟我 说， Julia 今天 跟 她 朋友 说 她 爱 他 吗？ 虽然 我 真的 不想 跟他 说话， 但是 我 喷嚏了 两次 就 跟他说：「什么事？ 」

「什么事？ 什么事 呢？ 我 完蛋了。 你 要 帮我忙！ 」

我 想 （但是 没有 跟他 说） ， 我 已经 帮了 他 很多 忙。 他 还要 我 做 什么？ 要我 唱 歌 给她 听 吗？ 要我 亲吻 她 吗？

好了， 亲吻 不会 这麽 糟糕…

「Josh！ Julia 要 跟我 吃 中饭！ 我 怎麽 办？ 我 真的 完蛋了！ 」Josh 的 眼睛 很大，脸 都 红色。 我 向他 翻了 眼。

「你 坐 吧。 你 还好 吗？ 要不要 喝 水？」 我 喷嚏 了。

「喷嚏 的人 是你， 而 不是 我。」 他 打了 我的 头。 「我 不想 喝水！ 我 要你 再 帮我 忙， 好吗？ 她 要 跟我 吃 中饭。 如果 我 跟

dishízhāng

yīge xīngqīsì, wǒ zài xuéxiào cāntīng deshíhòu, jiù tīngdàole Christian. tā zài jiào wǒde míngzì. "Josh! Josh!"

zāogāo. tā shìbúshì yào gēnwǒ shuō, Julia jīntiān gēn tā péngyǒu shuō tā ài tā ma? suīrán wǒ zhēnde bùxiǎng gēntā shuōhuà, dànshì wǒ pēntìle liǎngcì jiù gēntāshuō: "shénme shì?"

"shénme shì? shénme shì ne? wǒ wándànle. nǐ yào bāngwǒ máng!"

wǒ xiǎng (dànshì méiyǒu gēntā shuō), wǒ yǐjīng bāngle tā hěnduō máng. tā háiyào wǒ zuò shénme? yào wǒ chànggē gěi tā tīng ma? yào wǒ qīnwěn tā ma?

hǎole, qīnwěn búhuì zhème zāogāo...

"Josh! Julia yào gēnwǒ chī zhōngfàn! wǒ zěnme bàn? wǒ zhēnde wándànle!" Josh de yǎnjīng hěn dà, liǎn dōu hóngsè. wǒ xiàng tā fānle yǎn.

"nǐ zuò ba. nǐ háihǎo ma? yàobúyào hē shuǐ?" wǒ pēntì le.

"pēntì de rén shì nǐ, ér búshì wǒ." tā dǎle wǒdetóu. "wǒ bùxiǎng hēshuǐ! wǒ yào nǐ zài bāngwǒ máng, hǎoma? tā yào gēnwǒ chī

她 说话，她 就 会 知道，信 不是 我 写的。我 没办法 跟 她 说话。你 知道！我 怎麽 办？完蛋了！」

我 给 他 一瓶 水。虽然 他 不想 喝水，但是 喝水 的 人 不能 说话。我 不太 想要 听 Josh 说话 了。「你 喝水 吧！」

Josh 很快 就 把水 喝完了。「我 怎麽办？」

「怎麽办？跟 她 说话 吧！」Josh 摇了 头，但是 都 没有 说话。「她 是 一个 女孩子，你 每天 都 跟 女孩子 说话！」

他 摇头 摇得 更快。「不行！我 不行！她 马上 就 会 知道 那些信 不是 我 写的。我 完蛋了！」

我 没有 说话。Josh 看了 看我。在 餐厅 的 学生 很多。在 右边，我 看到了 Billy Heller 跟 一个 很 不高兴 的 学生 说话。我 看了 Christian。他 真的 帮了 我 很大的 忙。

没办法。我 喷嚏 了。

Christian 看了 我。「你 怎麽 喷嚏 这麽 多？那麽 你 会 帮我忙，不是 吗？」

「好了。下课 的 时候，你 来 我 的 家。我们 要 想 办法。」

zhōngfàn.

rúguǒ wǒ gēntā shuōhuà, tā jiù huì zhīdào, xìn búshì wǒ xiěde. wǒ méibànfǎ gēn tā shuōhuà. nǐ zhīdào! wǒ zěnme bàn? wándànle!"

wǒ gěi tā yīpíng shuǐ. suīrán tā bùxiǎng hēshuǐ, dànshì hēshuǐ derén búnéng shuōhuà. wǒ bútài xiǎngyào tīng Josh shuōhuà le. "nǐ hēshuǐ ba!"

Josh hěnkuài jiù bǎ shuǐ hēwánle. "wǒ zěnme bàn?"

"zěnme bàn? gēntā shuōhuà ba!" Josh yáole tóu, dànshì dōu méiyǒu shuōhuà. tā shì yīge nǔháizǐ, nǐ měitiān dōu gēn nǔháizǐ shuōhuà! "

tā yáotóu yáode gèngkuài. "bùxíng! wǒ bùxíng! tā mǎshàng jiù huì zhīdào nàxiēxìn búshì wǒ xiěde. wǒ wándànle!"

wǒ méiyǒu shuōhuà. Josh kànlekàn wǒ. zài cāntīng de xuéshēng hěnduō. zài yòubiān, wǒ kàndàole Billy Heller gēn yīge hěn bùgāoxìng de xuéshēng shuōhuà. wǒ kànle Christian. tā zhēnde bāngle wǒ hěndàde máng.

méibànfǎ. wǒ pēntì le.

Christian kànle wǒ. "nī zěnme pēntì zhème duō? nàme nǐ huì bāngwǒmáng, búshì ma?"

"hǎole. xiàkè deshíhòu, nǐ lái wǒde jiā. wǒmen yào xiǎng bànfǎ."

Chapter Eleven

　　第二天，Christian 很紧张。我跟他说没有问题，但是他还很紧张。

　　「我心理很怕！如果你听不见，我怎麽办？如果耳机不行怎麽办？」他不高兴地摇了头。「如果——」

　　「Christian，我就会在餐厅里面。你会听得见。耳机不会有问题。不要这样，好不好？那麼，麦克风你有吗？」

　　「就在这儿。」我看到了很小的、黑色的麦克风在他的衬衫下。

　　「那就没有问题了。麦克风在你的衬衫下。我会听得见你们说话。你有耳机吗？」

　　Christian 打开了他的背包。「有。耳机就在这儿。」

　　我点了头。「好。不要忘记！如果你有问题，还是不知道你要说什么，你要摸一摸头髮。如果你摸你的头髮，我会再说一遍。好不好？」

　　Christian 紧张地说：「好。」他的声音

dìshiyīhāng

dìèrtiān, Christian hěn jǐnzhāng. wǒ gēntā shuō méiyǒu wèntí, dànshì tā hái hěn jǐnzhāng.

"wǒ xīnlǐ hěn pà! rúguǒ nǐ tīngbújiàn, wǒ zěnme bàn? rúguǒ ěrjī bùxíng zěnmebàn?" tā bùgāoxìngde yáoletóu. "rúguǒ..."

"Christian! wǒ jiù huì zài cāntīng lǐmiàn. nǐ huì tīngdejiàn. ěrjī búhuì yǒu wèntí. búyào zhèyang, hǎobùhǎo? nàme, màikèfēng nǐ yǒu ma?"

"jiù zài zhèr." wǒ kàndàole hěnxiǎode, hēisède màikèfēng zài tāde chènshān xià.

"nà jiù méiyǒu wèntí le. màikèfēng zài nǐde chènshān xià. wǒ huì tīngdejiàn nǐmen shuōhuà. nǐ yǒu ěrjī ma?"

Christian dǎkāile tāde bēibāo. "yǒu. ěrijī jiù zài zhèr."

wǒ diǎnle tóu. "hǎo. búyào wàngjì! rúguǒ nǐ yǒu wèntí, háishì bùzhīdào nǐ yào shuō shénme, nǐ yào mōyīmō tóufa. rúguǒ nǐ mō nǐde tóufa, wǒ huì zàishuōyībiān. hǎobùhǎo?"

Christian jǐnzhāngde shuō: "hǎo." tāde

不强。他的脸很白。「我…我觉得我会呕吐。」

「不要呕吐!」我看了我的手表。「快十二点钟了。加油!」我走开了。

我看 Christian 坐下。他没有买中饭。他坐在那儿左看右看，很紧张。我小声跟他说：「如果你听得见，摸一下头髮。」他的手满满地摸了他的头髮。「好。」

他都在摸头髮。「好了!不要摸了!」他太紧张了!但是他就不摸了。

两分钟以後，Julia 就在那儿坐下了。哎哟，她好好看!我真的可以帮 Christian 说好听的话吗?我摇了头。我要。我跟他说我会帮他说话。没办法。

我看了他们两个人。没有人说话。「Christian，你要说什么!」

「什么。」

Julia 看了看 Christian.「你说什么?」

「对。」

我翻了眼睛。「Christian，跟她说她今天穿的衣服很好看。」

「她今天穿的衣服很好看。」

shēngyīn bùqiáng. tāde liǎn hěnbái. "wǒ...wǒ
juéde wǒ huì ǒutù."

"búyào ǒutù!" wǒ kànle wǒde shǒubiǎo.
"kuài shíèrdiǎnzhōng le. jiāyóu!" wǒ zǒukāile.

wǒkàn Christian zuòxià. tā méiyǒu mǎi
zhōngfàn. tā zuòzài nàr zuǒkànyòukàn, hěn
jǐnzhāng. wǒ xiǎoshēng gēn tā shuō: "rúguǒ
nǐ tīngbdejiàn, mōyīxià tóufa." tāde shǒu
mànmānde mōle tāde tóufa. "hǎo."

tā dōu zài mōtóufa. "hǎole! búyào mōle!" tā
tài jǐnzhāngle! dànshì tā jiù bù mōle.

liǎngfēnzhōng yǐhòu, Julia jiù zài nàr
zuòxiàle. āiyō, tā hǎo hǎokàn! wǒ zhēnde kěyǐ
bāng Christian shuō hǎotīngde huà ma? wǒ
yáole tóu. wǒ yào. wǒ gēntā shuō wǒ huì bāng
tā shuōhuà. méibànfǎ.

wǒ kànle tāmen liǎngge rén. méiyǒu rén
shuōhuà. "Christian! nǐ yào shuō shénme!"

"shénme."

Julia kànlekàn Christian. "nǐ shuō shénme?"

"duì."

wǒ fānle yǎnjīng. "Christian! gēntā shuō tā
jīntiān chuānde yīfu hěnhǎokàn."

"tā jīntiān chuānde yīfu hěnhǎokàn."

Julia 跟他 说：「谁？ 你说 谁的 衣服 好 看？」

哎哟。 Christian 怎麼 这麼 笨？ 「Christian， 你的 衣服 好看。」

「你 为什麼 说 我的 衣服？」Christian 摸 了 他的 头髮。

Julia 看他 摸头髮。「你 怎麼 了？ 你说 衣 服， 现在 你 摸头髮。 你 怎麼 了？」

「没事， 没事。」

她 看了看 Christian。 「你 不吃 中饭 吗？」

Christian 又 摸了 头髮。 「我…我…」

「你的 头 癢了 吗？」

「不会， 就是…」

Julia 看了我。 她 为什麼 要 看我？ 我 很 快 就 看了 我的 背包。

「你 是不是 没有 洗头？」

Christian 开了 口， 但是 没有 说话。 他 又 摸了 头髮。 我 怎麼 帮他？ 我 说什麼， 他 都 不懂。 真 麻烦！

「Christian， 跟 她 说：『我 看到 你 的 时 候， 我 就 是 牛郎 看 织女。』」

Julia gēn tā shuō: "shéi? nǐshuō shéide yīfu hǎokàn?"

āiyō. Christian zěnme zhème bèn?

"Christian, nǐde yīfu hǎokàn." "nǐ wèishénme shuō wǒde yīfu?" Christian mōle tāde tóufa.

Julia kàn tā mōtóufa. "nǐ zěnme le? nǐ shuō yīfu, xiànzài nǐ mōtóufa. nǐ zěnme le?"

"méishì, méishì."

tā kànlekàn Christian. "nǐ bùchī zhōngfàn ma?"

Christian yòu mōle tóufa. "wǒ...wǒ..."

"nǐde tóu yǎngle ma?"

"búhuì! jiùshì…"

Julia kànle wǒ. tā wèishénme yào kàn wǒ? wǒ hěnkuài jiù kànle wǒde bēibāo.

"nǐ shìbúshì méiyǒu xǐtóu?"

Christian kāile kǒu, dànshì méiyǒu shuōhuà. tā yòu mōle tóufa. wǒ zěnme bāng tā? wǒ shuō shénme, tā dōu bùdǒng. zhēn máfán!

"Christian! gēn tā shuō: 'wǒ kàndào nǐ deshíhòu, wǒ jiù shì níláng kàn zhīnǚ.' "

「我看到你的时候，我就是 Nolan 看⋯看谁？」

Julia 跟 Christian 说：「什么 Nolan？你不叫 Christian 吗？」

Christian 还在摸头髮。「那是什么？是耳机吗？你不想跟我说话吗？如果你想听音乐，我就跟朋友吃中饭。」

「我不是⋯那就是说⋯」

但是 Julia 走了。

我看了看 Christian。他快要哭了。他都坐在那儿。很多同学都在看他。同学都走来走去，但是 Christian 都一个人在那儿。

"wǒ kàndào nǐ deshíhòu, wǒ jiùshì nolan kàn...kàn shéi?"

Julia gēn Christian shuō: "shénme nolan? nǐ bújiào Christian ma?"

Christian hái zài mōtóufa. nàshì shénme? shì ěrjī ma? nǐ bù xiǎng gēn wǒ shuōhuà ma? rúguǒ nǐ xiǎng tīng yīnyuè, wǒ jiù gēn péngyǒu chīzhōngfàn."

"wǒ búshì...nà jiùshì shuō..."

 dànshì Julia zǒule.

wǒ kànlekàn Christian. tā kuàiyào kūle. tā dōu zuòzài nàr. hěnduō tóngxué dōu zài kàntā. tóngxué dōu zǒuláizǒuqù, dànshì Christian dōu yīgerén zài nàr.

Chapter Twelve

第二天，Christian 不跟我 说话。我 要去上 历史课 的时候 才 看到了 他。

「你 怎麼了？有了 小小的 麻烦，但是 你不可以 那样！」

Christian 看了 我，但是 没有 说话。

「好了。好了。我 不 知道 你 为什麽 要生 我的 气。你 要 我 帮你，我 就 帮了 你忙。我 可以 做的，我 都 做了！」他 没有说话，只生气地 看了 我。

「好了，我 要 去 上课。我 跟你 没办法！」

历史课 过得 很慢。我 都 在 看 Julia 黑色的 头髮。我 为什麽 不可以 跟她 说话了？Christian 有了 机会。他 就是 没办法 跟Julia说话。我 给了 Christian 很好的 机会。我 什麼时候 有 机会？如果 我 不是 跟 Julia 说话，我 为什麽 学了 中文？

对了。我 要 跟她 说话。

快要 下课 的时候，我 才 开了 口 跟 我的天使 说话。老师 是 跟 一个 同学 说话。那就是 我的 机会 了！

dìshíèrzhāng

dìèrtiān, Christian bù gēn wǒ shuōhuà. wǒ yào qùshàng lìshǐkè deshíhòu cái kàndàole tā.

"nǐ zěnme le? yǒule xiǎoxiǎode máfán, dànshì nǐ bùkěyǐ nàyàng!"

Christian kànle wǒ, dànshì méiyǒu shuōhuà.

" hǎole. hǎole. wǒ bù zhīdào nǐ wèishénme yào shēng wǒde qì. nǐ yào wǒ bangmáng, wǒ jiù bāngle nǐ máng. wǒ kěyǐ zuòde, wǒ dōu zuòle! tā méiyǒu gēntā shuōhuà, zhǐ shēngqìde kànle wǒ.

"hǎole, wǒ yào qù shàngkè. wǒ gēnnǐ méibànfǎ!"

lìshǐkè guòde hěnmàn. wǒ dōu zài kàn Julia hēisède tóufa. wǒ wèishénme bùkěyǐ gēntā shuōhuà le? Christian yǒule jīhuì. tā jiùshì méibànfǎ gēn Julia shuōhuà. wǒ gěilē Christian hěnhǎode jīhuì. wǒ shénmeshíhòu yǒu jīhuì? rúguǒ wǒ búshì gēn Julia shuōhuà, wǒ wèishénme xuéle zhōngwén?

duìle. wǒ yào gēntā shuōhuà.

kuàiyào xiàkè deshíhòu, wǒ cái kāile kǒu gēn wǒde tiānshǐ shuōhuà. lǎoshī shì gēn yīge tóngxué shuōhuà. nà jiùshì wǒde jīhuì le!

「Julia你好我很久就想跟你说话但是现在才有机会你很独一无二我很喜欢你不知道--」

我 跟 她 说了 话！她 在 看我！我 看得到 她的 咖啡色的 眼睛。我怕 我会 呕吐！

Julia 跟我 说：「你 说什么？」

我 用 英文 跟她说：「是 中文。我 喜欢 你，所以 我 学了 中文。」我 就 没有 话说 了。

Julia 笑了。「哎哟！」她 摇了 头。她 还 是 跟我 说 英文。「很 可惜！」

「可惜吗？你 不喜欢 我吗？」

「不是 不喜欢 你。你 很 不错。但是，有 两个 小麻烦。第一，我们 家 说 广东话。我 不会 说 普通话。」

她 说我 不错！「我 可以 学！没问题！我 明天 就 去 找 老师！」

Julia 摇了 头。「不好意思...但是 还有…我 们 下个 星期 就要 回 中国 了。」

我 失望了 吗？很失望。Christian 生 我的

"Julia nǐhǎowǒhěnjiǔjiùxiǎnggēnnǐshuōhuàd ànshìxiànzàicáiyǒujīhuìnǐhěndúyīwúèrwǒhěnxǐh uānnǐbùzhīdào..."

wǒ gēntā shuōle huà! tā zài kàn wǒ! wǒ kàndedào tāde kāfēisède yǎnjīng. wǒpà wǒhuì ǒutù!

Julia gēn wǒ shuō: "nǐ shuō shénme?"

wǒ yòng yīngwén gēntā shuó: "shì zhōngwén. wǒ xǐhuān nǐ, suǒyǐ wǒ xuéle zhōngwén." wǒ jiù méiyǒu shuōhuà le.

Julia xiàole. "āiyō!" tā yáole tóu, tā háishì gēn wǒ shuō yīngwén. hěn kěxí!

"kěxí ma? nǐ bù xǐhuān wǒ ma?"

"búshì bù xǐhuān nǐ. nǐ hěn búcuò. dànshì, yǒu liǎngge xiǎomáfán. dìyī, wǒmen jiā shuō guǎngdōnghuà. wǒ búhuì shuō pǔtōnghuà."

tā shuō wǒ búcuò! "wǒ kěyǐ xué! méi wèntí! wǒ míngtiān jiù qù zhǎo lǎoshī!"

Julia yáole tóu. bùhǎoyìsi...dànshì háiyǒu... wǒmen xiàgexīngqī jiùyào huí zhōngguóle."

----

wǒ shīwàngle ma? hěn shīwàng. Christian shēng wǒde qī. wǒ xǐhuānde nǚháizǐ yào huí

气。我 喜欢的 女孩子 要 回 中国 了。当然 我 不 高兴。这些 都 不好。

但是 也 有 好的。我 爸爸 妈妈 知道 我 在 上网 学 中文，他们 很 高兴。他们 说，学 好 中文，可能 帮我 上 大学。大学 很 贵，但是 如果 我 学好 中文，我 有 可能 去 中国 上 大学。

还有，Julia 走 以前，她 跟我 要了 我的 email。她说，虽然 她 在家 说 广东话，但是 她 普通话 看得懂...

我 开了 电脑。「Bubba 老师 好！今天 学 什麼 呢？」

zhōngguó le. dāngrán wǒ bù gāoxìng. zhèxiē
dōu bùhǎo.

dànshì yě yǒu hǎode. wǒ bàba māma zhīdào
wǒ zài shàngwǎng xué zhōngwén, tāmen hěn
gāoxìng. tāmen shuō, xuéhǎo zhōngwén, kěnéng
bāngwǒ shàng dàxué. dàxué hěnguì, dànshì
rúguǒ wǒ xuéhǎo zhōngwén, wǒ yǒu kěnéng qù
zhōngguó shàng dàxué.

hāiyóu, Julia zǒu yǐqián, tā gēnwǒ yàole
wǒde email. tā shuō, suīrán tā zài jiā shuō
guǎngdōnghuà, dōu tīngbùdǒng pǔtōnghuà,
dànshì tā pǔtōnghuà kàndedǒng…

wǒ kāile diànnǎo. "bubba lǎoshī hǎo! jīntiān
wǒmen xué shénme ne?"

Glossary

Numbers in parentheses indicate chapter where the word first appears

ǎi, 矮: short (height) (2)

ài, 爱: love (3)

àishàng, 爱上: fall in love with (3)

bāxī, 巴西: Brazil (5)

bǎ, 把: (marks the object of the sentence) (3)

bàba, 爸爸: daddy (2)

ba, 吧: (suggestion) (1)

báirén, 白人: white person (3)

bàituo, 拜託: do-this-for-me (8)

bànfǎ, 办法: way to do something (1)

bāng, 帮: help (7)

bāngmáng, 帮忙: help (7)

bāngtāmáng, 帮他忙: help him (9)

bēibāo, 背包: backpack (1)

běnlái, 本来: originally (7)

bèn, 笨: stupid (1)

bǐ, 比: compared to (1)

bǐ, 笔: pen (1)

biérén, 别人: other people (6)

bīngdǎoyǔ, 冰岛语: Icelandic language (5)

cái, 才: then-and-only-then (1)

cāntīng, 餐厅: restaurant (10)

chángtóufǎ, 长头髮: long hair (9)

chànggē, 唱歌: sing a song (10)

chènshān, 衬衫: shirt (11)

chūqù, 出去: go out (6)

chǔwùguì, 储物柜: locker (1)

dǎ, 打: hit (1)

dǎkāi, 打开: open up (1)

dà, 大: big (2)

dàjiā, 大家: everyone (2)

dàshēng, 大声: loud voice, loudly (6)

dàxué, 大学: university (12)

dāngrán, 当然: of course (4)

dào, 到: arrive (1)

déwén, 德文: German language (5)

de, 得: in a way that is... (1)

de, 的: 's; one that is... (1)

derén, 的人: a person that is... (10)

deshíhòu, 的时候: at the time when... (1)

děng, 等: wait (1)

děngdào, 等到: wait until (1)

dìdi, 弟弟: little brother (2)

dìfāng, 地方: place (2)

dìyī, 第一: first (12)

dìyījié, 第一节: first period (3)

dìyītiān, 第一天: the first day (2)

diànnǎo, 电脑: computer (5)

diànyǐng, 电影: movie (7)

dōngxī, 东西: thing (1)

dōu, 都: all; both (1)

dúyīwúèr, 独一无二: unique; special (4)

duì, 对: correct (5)

duìle, 对了: oh, right! (I forgot before...) (5)

duō, 多: a lot of; numerous (1)

duōcháng, 多长: how long? (4)

duōjiǔ, 多久: how long? (1)

duōkànle, 多看了: read/look a bit more (8)

duōshǎo, 多少: how much? (1)

ér, 而: but rather (6)

érbúshì, 而不是: and not (9)

érshì, 而是: but rather is (9)

ěrjī, 耳机: earphones; head-phones (11)

fǎwén, 法文: French language (5)

fǎyǔ, 法语: French language (spoken) (1)

fānle, 翻了: rolled; turned over (10)

fánnǎo, 烦恼: irritated (1)

fángjiān, 房间: room (9)

fàngzài, 放在: put (in a place) (9)

fēicháng, 非常: extremely (3)

fùmǔ, 父母: parents (2)

gǎnlǎnqiú, 橄榄球: (American) football (1)

gǎnmào, 感冒了: catch cold (9)

gāo, 高: tall (2)

gāoshǒu, 高手: expert (3)

gāosì, 高四: senior in high school (2)

gāosìxuéshēng, 高四学生: senior (2)

gāoxìng, 高兴: happy (1)

gāoyī, 高一: 1st year high school (2)

gāozhōng, 高中: high school (2)

"gǎosǐ, 搞死: ""to cause death"" (2)"

gěi, 给: give; to/for (3)

gēn, 跟: with (1)

gēntāshuō, 跟她说: said to him (9)

gēnwǒ, 跟我: to/with me (1)

gēnwǒshuō, 跟我说: said to me (2)

gèngduōde, 更多的: even more of (6)

gèngjǐnzhāng, 更紧张: even more nervous (6)

gèngmáfánde, 更麻烦的: even more irritating (6)

gōngkè, 功课: homework (1)

gōngzuò, 工作: work; job (2)

gǒu, 狗: dog (2)

guāndiào, 关掉: turn off (6)

guānxi, 关係: connection (1)

guǎn, 管: manage (6)

guǎnwǒdeshì, 管我的事: take care of my business (6)

guǎngdōnghuà, 广东话: Can-tonese (12)

guì, 贵: expensive (5)

guòde, 过得: passed in a way that was... (12)

hái, 还: still (1)

háihǎo, 还好: not bad (1)

háishì, 还是: or (11)

háishì, 还是: or (3)

háiyǒu, 还有: there is still... (1)

hànbǎobāo, 汉堡包: hamburger (4)

hǎo, 好: good; be good (2)

hǎohǎokàn, 好好看: very nice-looking (11)

hǎole, 好了: fine then (1)

hǎoyòng, 好用: useful (2)

hàoma, 号码: number (1)

hē, 喝: drink (10)

hēshuǐ, 喝水: drink water (10)

hēwánle, 喝完了: drank up (10)

hé, 和: and (between 2 nouns) (2)

hēi, 黑: black (1)

hēirén, 黑人: black person (3)

hēisè, 黑色: black (3)

hěn, 很: very (1)

hěnbèn, 很笨: really stupid (8)

hěnbúcuò, 很不错: not bad at all (6)

hěnhóng, 很红: really popular

hěntòng, 很痛: hurts a lot (1)

hěnwúliáo, 很无聊: really boring (5)

hóngsè, 红色: red (10)

huà, 话: speech (3)

huàhuà, 画画: draw a picture (1)

huàxuékè, 化学课: chemistry class (1)

huí, 回: go back to (9)

huíjiā, 回家: go back home (1)

huì, 会: able to; likely to (1)

huìwèn hěnduō wèntí, 会问很多问题: would ask a lot of questions (6)

jī, 鸡: chicken (2)

jīhuì, 机会: opportunity (12)

jǐcì, 几次: several times (1)

jǐdiǎnzhōng, 几点钟: what time? (1)

jǐge, 几个: several (8)

jǐhǎole, 挤好了: all milked (4)

jǐnǎi, 挤奶: to milk (2)

jǐnǎijī, 挤奶机: milking machine (2)

jiā, 家: home (2)

jiārén, 家人: family (2)

jiāyóu, 加油: go team! (11)

jiǎo, 脚: foot (1)

jiào, 叫: call; yell (2)

jiàoliàn, 教练: coach (2)

jiàozhōngwén, 教中文: teach Chinese (5)

jīnnián, 今年: this year (2)

jīnsè, 金色: golden colored (4)

jǐnzhāng, 紧张: nervous (11)

jiǔ, 久: a long time (1)

jiǔniánjí, 九年级: ninth grade (2)

jiù, 就: precisely; sooner-than-expected (1)

juédé, 觉得: feel (11)

kāishǐ, 开始: begin (1)

kàn, 看: look at (2)

kànbújiàn, 看不见: cannot be seen (1)

kàndào, 看到: see (1)

kàndedào, 看得到: able to see (12)

kàndedǒng, 看得懂...: able to read and understand (12)

kàndiànyǐng, 看电影: watch a movie (7)

kàndǒng, 看懂: read and understand (8)

kànxìn, 看信: read a letter (9)

kànyīkàn, 看一看: take a look at (4)

kǎode, 考得: took a test in a way that was... (9)

kǎoshì, 考试: take a test (7)

kēxuékè, 科学课: science class (3)

kěyǐ, 可以: is permitted to, can (1)

kè, 课: class (3)

kèběn, 课本: textbook (1)

kǒu, 口: mouth (11)

kū, 哭: cry (1)

kuài, 快: fast (1)

kuàiyào, 快要: will soon (1)

lādīngwén, 拉丁文: Latin language (5)

làmèi, 辣妹: hot chick (8)

lái, 来: come (1)

lánqiú, 篮球: basketball (2)

lánsè, 蓝色: blue (5)

lǎoshī, 老师: teacher (1)

lèile, 累了: tired (1)

lěngle, 冷了: got cold (9)

lǐmiàn, 里面: inside (1)

lìshǐ, 历史: history (3)

liǎn, 脸: face (1)
liǎnhóng, 脸红: face is red (7)
liǎnhóngle, 脸红了: blushed (7)
liǎojiě, 瞭解: understand (6)
máfán, 麻烦: irritating, bothersome (1)
mǎshàng, 马上: immediately (10)
ma, 吗: yes-or-no? (1)
mǎi, 买: buy (5)
mài, 卖: sell (5)
màikèfēng, 麦克风: microphone (11)
mànmānde, 满满地: slowly (11)
máng, 忙: busy (6)
māo, 猫: cat (2)
méicuò, 没错: that's right (2)
méiguānxi, 没关係: it doesn't matter (4)
méishénme, 没甚麼: it's nothing (8)
méishì, 没事: there's nothing wrong (11)
méiwèntí, 没问题: there's no problem (12)
méiyǒu, 没有: there isn't; don't have (1)
méiyǒuguānxi, 没有关係: it doesn't matter (3)
méiyǒurén, 没有人: no one (1)
měi, 美: beautiful (3)
měiguó, 美国: USA (2)
měiguórén, 美国人: American (3)
měinv3, 美女: beautiful woman (3)
měitiān, 每天: every day (9)
mén, 门: door (1)
míngtiān, 明天: tomorrow (7)
míngtiānjiàn, 明天见: see you tomorrow (8)

míngxīng, 明星: star (2)
míngzì, 名字: name (2)
mō, 摸: rub (11)
mōyīmō, 摸一摸: rub a little (11)
mōyīxià, 摸一下: rub a little (11)
ná, 拿: take with the hand (1)
nábúdào, 拿不到: cannot reach (1)
nà / nèi, 那: that (1)
nàèr, 那儿: there (4)
nàge, 那个: that one (1)
nàwèi, 那位: that (person) (3)
nàxiē, 那些: those (9)
nán, 难: difficult (8)
nánháizǐ, 男孩子: boy (3)
nánrén, 男人: man (1)
ne, 呢: (softens a statement) (1)
nián, 年: year (7)
niú, 牛: cow (2)
niúláng, 牛郎: Cowboy (in Chinese myth) (11)
nóngchǎng, 农场: farm (2)
nv3háizǐ, 女孩子: girl (1)
nv3rén, 女人: woman (1)
ǒutù, 呕吐: vomit (11)
pà, 怕: be afraid of (11)
pēntì, 喷嚏: sneeze (9)
pēng, 砰: bang! (pounding sound on metal) (1)
péngyǒu, 朋友: friend (2)
pīsà, 披萨: pizza (4)
pùtōnghuà, 普通话: Mandarin Chinese (12)
qīdiǎn, 七点: seven o'clock (1)
qīniánjí, 七年级: seventh grade (2)
qíguài, 奇怪: strange (7)
qián, 钱: money (5)
qiánbāo, 钱包: purse; wallet (1)
qiánmiàn, 前面: front (1)
qīnwěn, 亲吻: kiss (10)

qǐng, 请: please; to invite (7)

qùnián, 去年: last year (4)

ránhòu, 然後: afterwards, then (1)

ràng, 让: to make someone (feel a certain way) (4)

rènshi, 认识: to know a person (2)

ròuguī, 肉桂: cinnamon (4)

rúguǒ, 如果: if (1)

shàngwǎng, 上网: go on the INternet (12)

shǎo, 少: few (2)

shéi, 谁: who? (1)

shēntǐ, 身体: health; body (9)

shénme, 什么: what (2)

shénme shíhòu, 什麼时候: when? (6)

shēngqì, 生气: get angry (3)

shēngyīn, 声音: noise; voice (6)

shīwàng, 失望: disappointed (9)

shì, 是: is, be, am, are... (1)

shǒu, 手: hand (1)

shǒubiǎo, 手表: wristwatch (11)

shǒuzhōngde, 手中的: the one in the hand (9)

shùxué, 数学: math (3)

shuǐ, 水: water (10)

shuō, 说: speak (1)

shuōcuò, 说错: to say something wrong (7)

shuōhuà, 说话: to talk (1)

sīwāxīlǐyǔ, 斯瓦希里语: Swahili language (5)

sǐdìngle, 死定了: dead for sure (6)

suīrán, 虽然: although (1)

suǒyǐ, 所以: therefore (1)

tā, 她: she (1)

tābúyàoqián, 他不要钱: he doesn't want money; he's free (6)

tāde, 她的: her (1)

tāmen, 她们: they (females) (7)

táifēng, 台风: hurricane (6)

tài, 太: too (1)

tàiduōle, 太多了: too much (2)

tèbié, 特别: special (1)

tī, 踢: kick (1)

tīgǎnlǎnqiú, 踢橄榄球: play football (2)

tīgǎnlǎnqiú tīde, 踢橄榄球踢得: play football well (4)

tīrén, 踢人: kick someone (2)

tǐyùkè, 体育课: phys ed class (3)

tiānqì, 天气: weather (9)

tiānshǐ, 天使: angel (12)

tīng, 听: listen to (1)

tīngbújiàn, 听不见: listen but not hear (11)

tīngbùdǒng, 听不懂: listen but don't understand (12)

tīngbùdǒng, 听不懂: listen but not understand (1)

tīngdào, 听到: hear (1)

tīngdejiàn, 听得见: able to hear (11)

tīngshuō, 听说: hear it said that... (3)

tóngxué, 同学: classmate (2)

tòng, 痛: painful (1)

tóu, 头: head (3)

tóufǎ, 头髮: hair (3)

tóutòng, 头痛: headache (1)

túshūguǎn, 图书馆: library (7)

tuǐ, 腿: leg (1)

wài, 外: outside (1)

wàimiàn, 外面: outside (1)

wándànle, 完蛋了: dead duck (10)

wǎnfàn, 晚饭: dinner (9)

wǎnshàng, 晚上: evening (1)

wǎngzhàn, 网站: web site (5)

wàngjì, 忘记: forget (11)

wàngle, 忘了: forgot (6)

wèidào, 味道: scent; flavor (4)

wèishénme, 为什麼: why? (1)

wèn, 问: ask (6)

wèntí, 问题: question; problem (2)

wǒ, 我: I, me (1)

wǒdeshì, 我的事: my business (6)

wǒmen, 我们: we, us (1)

wòshì, 卧室: bedroom (5)

wúliáo, 无聊: boring (1)

wǔfēngxìn, 五封信: five letters (9)

xībānyáqiáo, 西班牙侨: Hispanic person (3)

xībānyáwén, 西班牙文: Spanish language (5)

xībānyáyǔ, 西班牙语: Spanish language (spoken) (4)

xǐhuān, 喜欢: like (1)

xǐhuānshàng, 喜欢上: like someone (4)

xǐtóu, 洗头: wash hair (11)

xiàkè, 下课: get out of class (12)

xiànzài, 现在: now (2)

xiāng, 香: fragrant (4)

xiāngcǎo, 香草: vanilla (4)

xiǎng, 想: think, feel like (doing something) (1)

xiǎngbànfǎ, 想办法: think of a way (9)

xiǎngdào, 想到: think of (3)

xiǎngyào, 想要: want to (6)

xiàngtā, 向他: toward him (10)

xiǎo, 小: small (1)

xiǎoshēng, 小声: quiet (11)

xiǎoshí, 小时: hour (7)

xiǎoxīn, 小心: be careful (2)

xiàole, 笑了: smiled; laughed (4)

xiàozhe, 笑着: smiling; laughing (9)

xiě, 写: write (8)

xiěde, 写得: write in a way that is... (9)

xiěhǎole, 写好了: finished writing, written (9)

xièxiè, 谢谢: thank you (3)

xīnde, 新的: new (3)

xīnlǐ, 心理: in (his/her) heart (11)

xīngqī, 星期: week (3)

xīngqīsān, 星期叁: Wednesday (7)

xìng, 姓: last name (is) (3)

xìngmíng, 姓名: full name (5)

xué, 学: study (1)

xuéhǎo, 学好: study and master (4)

xuéshēng, 学生: student (2)

xuéxiào, 学校: school (1)

yǎnjīng, 眼睛: eyes (1)

yǎng, 养: raise (animals, children...) (2)

yàngzi, 样子: way; appearance (1)

yáole, 摇了: shook (10)

yáoletóu, 摇了头: shook (his/her) head (11)

yào, 要: want; will; must (1)

yī cì, 一次: one time, occasion (6)

yī fēnzhōng, 一分钟: one minute (9)

yī píng, 一瓶: one bottle of (10)

yīfú, 衣服: clothing (3)

yíyàng, 一样: the same (2)

yǐhòu, 以後: after, afterwards (1)

yǐjīng, 已经: already (3)

yǐqián, 以前: before, previously (2)

yìjiàn, 意见: opinion (5)

yīnwèi, 因为: because (1)

yīnyuè, 音乐: music (11)

yīngwén, 英文: English language (1)

yòng, 用: use (1)

yònglì, 用力: use force (1)

yòngshǒu, 用手: use the hand (1)

yǒu, 有: have; there is/are (1)

yǒude, 有的: some (2)

yǒudeshíhòu, 有的时候: sometimes (7)

yǒurén, 有人: someone (1)

yǒuyītiān, 有一天: one day... (4)

yòu, 又: again (in the past) (6)

yòubiān, 右边: right side (10)

yuè, 越: the more... (9)

yuèkàn, 越看: the more (he) looked/read... (9)

zài, 再: again (in the future) (1)

zài, 在: be at (1)

zàijiā, 在家: be at home (1)

zàixiǎng, 在想: be thinking (1)

zāogāo, 糟糕: darn it! (10)

zěnměbàn, 怎麽办: what to do? (10)

zěnme, 怎麽: how (1)

zěnmele, 怎麽了: what is the problem? (7)

zhǎngde, 长得: grows to be... (2)

zhǎnggāo, 长高: grow up; grow tall (2)

zhǎo, 找: look for (12)

zhèr, 这儿: here (1)

zhège, 这个: this one (1)

zhème, 这麽: so (1)

zhèxiē, 这些: these (12)

zhèyàng, 这样: this way (6)

zhēn, 真: really (11)

zhī, 只: (measure word for animals) (2)

zhīdào, 知道: know (2)

zhīnǚ, 织女: Weaving Maid (Chinese mythology) (11)

zhǐ, 只: only (8)

zhōngfàn, 中饭: lunch (3)

zhōngguó, 中国: China (2)

zhōngwén, 中文: Chinese language (2)

zhū, 猪: pig (2)

zì, 字: character or letter (3)

zìwǒjièshào, 自我介绍: introduce myself (2)

zǒu, 走: walk (1)

zǒukāile, 走开了: walked away (11)

zǒuláizǒuqù, 走来走去: walk back and forth (11)

zǒule, 走了: went away (1)

zuì, 最: the most (6)

zuǒkànyòukàn, 左看右看: looking around (11)

zuò, 坐: sit (3)

zuòde, 做得: does in a way that is... (2)

zuòxià, 坐下: sit down (11)

zuòzài, 坐在: sits at/on (4)

CHINESE CARNIVAL
CHINESE CULTURE CARNIVAL

Set up your tents, book your acts, and watch out for your opponents' mischief, while wreaking a little havoc of your own! Whether you play in a group or solitaire, with others learning Chinese or in a mixed-subject game, Carnival is the fun way to make those new words and phrases really stick!

Real games. Real learning. Real fun.
www.SquidForBrains.com

SUNZI: GAME OF WAR

Set your sights on easily mastering the Chinese words you really need! Attack your opponent with the power of Chinese words. Choose from collection of decks focused on different aspects of Chinese learning and watch your vocabulary grow as you play.

Look for the companion decks for this book at www.SquidForBrains.com today!

Made in the USA
Middletown, DE
28 June 2015